For artists that are
starting from the bottom.

**Not the bottom of the rap game, like Drake
suggested in his uplifting and rousing anthemic song,
but rather starting from the** bottom of the creative ladder.

Gallery Walk-ins (UNSOLICITED)

Book Design: Victor Koroma
Editing: Alpha Wolfram

Contents "👑"

My Thoughts

(Unsolicited)

1.

(UNSOLICITED)

To the person reading this book, i must share something with you before we begin.

i'm refraining and omitting the use of capital "*I*'s" throughout this book. it's not because i'm ignorant of capitalization/grammar rules. it's simply because i enjoy the minimal architecture of lower case "*i*'s" more than i do capital "*I*'s." i'm letting you know this in advance, because i'm aware your eyes and educated mind will automatically try to cross them out and rewrite them as capital "*I*'s." i assure you they need no correction. it's just that i prefer, this (i) sound architecture instead. in fact, my love for lower case "*i*'s" neatly tie into this story, but you will find out more about it later on in our journey

Okay, the plan and concept of this book is rather simple. Well, at least in theory. The idea is to walk into ten galleries that don't accept unsolicited artist submissions and see what happens. This is not a random process. i'm specifically picking all the galleries that match the aesthetic of my work. Places i truly believe would be interested in my projects if they take the time to look. This is an experiment. This is performance art. My main goal is to walk-in. Witness their responses and write short stories about each individual experience. These short stories will be a contemporary depiction of what it's like to be in the shoes of a twenty-something-year-old artist attempting to get a gallery to unsolicitedly look at his work. Also, the term "walk-in" in the context of this book, means the process of walking into a gallery to unsolicitedly show them your artwork. Anyway, whether i get a show, or not, is not important. The aim is to shed light on this process while examining it.

i'm having fun and living life creatively.

Obviously, galleries don't encourage this form of contact. it goes against their rules. in fact, the words "The gallery does not accept unsolicited artist submissions" usually pops up screaming at you in full blaring volume. This message tends to swallow your hopes as you click on the contact pages on their websites. But art is about breaking the rules, right? And i don't need to be Duchamp or Warhol to break the rules, right? i just have to qualify as an artist on a mission to break some rule related to the art world, right? So why not break the "don't walk into our gallery and unsolicitedly show us your artwork" rule in a creative way?

What else is an eager artist to do?

Well, you're suppose to keep creating work until they notice you. Get a reference from either a curator, dealer, or an artist that's already with the gallery. And, you could always email them. But emails are impersonal. Realistically your email will just blend in and get lost in the hundreds of other emails they receive from other eager artists trying to break into the gallery world.

The way i see it, i have about a 99% chance of getting kicked out or turned away. And the 1% percent chance i have of getting a show or something happening is just my optimistic life belief that anything can happen. in short, this book is a documentation of my wildly entertaining, fascinating, uncomfortable, and awkward encounters.

This is an experiment, and i want to share my results with you.

This is a list of the things i'm bringing with me.

1. 4 x 48 white mailing tube that holds my 40 x 40 hand painted print on Moab Somerset Velvet Paper with deckled edges.

2. 11 x 14 frosted green glass portfolio that holds various bodies of work printed on inkpress Luster Paper.

3. One 8 x 10 aluminum metal print with a high gloss finish.

4. One 8 x 10 aluminum metal print with a brushed matte finish.

5. Two pairs of heavy white cotton gloves: a pair for me, and a pair for whoever is looking at my work.

2.

My Thoughts
(Smart Objects)

Gallery name — Smart Objects

Location — Echo Park, Los Angeles

Date — Friday, May 2, 2014

Lasted time frame — Approximately ten minutes

i look as if i'm delivering artwork. i'm walking past restaurants, coffee shops, record stores, and fashion boutiques. Eyes glance at me from all directions. it's either because they are intrigued by all the things i'm carrying, or because i look ridiculous carrying all these things.

i'm actually not nervous and wearing a calm facial expression. The main thoughts that keep bouncing around my head are "i can't believe your doing this!", "they are going think you're a crazy person that needs psychiatric help!!", and "run back to your car before its too late!!!"

i quiet my fears by telling them, "Shut up!" and push the glass door of a gray and whitish cement building. i'm greeted by the authoritative white gallery walls in there blinding glory. The space is empty except for the hanging art. As i begin to walk around, i hear a girl's voice from the back of the room warmly announcing, "Hi!"

The silence is broken. My instincts take over, and i walk over and introduce myself,

"Hey!" my name is Victor" - i shake her hand in a friendly manner. Make eye contact. Smile. She is sitting on a school chair, with a laptop resting on her lap. She has slick, jet-black hair, black-rimmed glasses, and a black dress with white stripes.

i enthusiastically say, "i came across your gallery online. i'm wondering if you'll take a look at my work and maybe i could be considered for an upcoming group show?" instantaneously her whole body language and welcoming buddy-buddy demeanor changes. i just dropped a verbal atomic bomb. She readjusts herself on the chair. Acts as if i just asked her out on a date, or worse - to make love to her on the cold gray cement floors of the gallery. As if i just told her what isaac (Woody Allen) said to Mary (Diane Keaton) in one of my favorite films of his, "Manhattan" - "i have a mad impulse to throw you down on the lunar surface and commit interstellar perversion with you".

Her face twitches. Her body continues to fidget around. Her eyes dart from spot. To spot. To spot. Finally, she responds, "Uh... i'm just an intern, and the curator isn't here right now. He has a specific eye for what he wants to include in his shows. He is interested in new artists, but we usually don't like walk-ins like this. Um... how about you email us saying exactly what you want to exhibit in our space and we will take it from there. i don't mind taking a look at your work, but the decision is not up to me."

Her eyes blink rapidly and she asks, "Are you in school?" i say, "i graduated a while ago. i just moved here from the east coast. i exhibit my work in gallery shows from time to time, but i'm still trying to spread my work around as much as possible."

i reach in my faux leather messenger bag and pull out my 11 x 14 frosted green glass portfolio. i can tell that she is still uneasy and doesn't really know what to say.

i take over the conversation, in order to make her feel comfortable again. i ask, "how long has the space been open?" "A year or so," she responds and as i ask, "Do you do any art yourself?" "- i paint, but i want to be a writer."

i hand her my portfolio as i explain various details to her. Things, like that i'm a photographer who creates images that look like paintings and illustrations. That i transform everyday objects beyond their banality, so people will think of them in new ways. i ask, "Do you think the work fits in with what you guys show here?" She responds, "i think the high gloss images work. They are very, "post-internet."

She says, "Do you know what that means?" i respond, "No. This is the first time i've heard that term, what is it?" Her face twitches and her eyes dart around as if in search for an answer. Her gaze returns to mine. She unleashes two words, "Google it." i tell her, "sure" - and find it amusing that she just used a term she couldn't define.

When she's done with my portfolio i had her my aluminum metal prints. She says, "These are cool." i say, "Thanks" - and mentally decide its probably not the best idea to take out my 40 x 40 hand painted print, because it will be too much of a hassle and there is no place to safely unroll it.

i put away my work. Say thank you and tell her that i'll email the website. i shake her hand. Make eye contact, and warmly say goodbye.

i walk out the building, and the sun is bright and shining. i think to myself, "That wasn't so bad... at least she looked at my work. And i did get a short story out of it. And if anything, i just made her day a little more interesting. She can tell her friends and co-workers about the artist that walked in today with all his artwork."

— —

Manhattan. Dir. Woody Allen. By Woody Allen, Marshall Brickman, and Gordon Willis. Prod. Charles H. Joffe. Perf. Woody Allen, Diane Keaton, Michael Murphy, Mariel Hemingway, Meryl Streep, and Anne Byrne Kronenfeld. United Artists Corporation, 1979. DVD.

What i learned from this gallery visit.

Galleries still don't appreciate "unsolicited artists submissions".

The curator might not be there. The person you will probably end up talking to is a slightly scared intern. Have an idea of exactly what you want to exhibit in the space, if you do get a chance to talk to someone. Be friendly and act kind. Have fun with it. Live creatively. it's performance art. You can invent a character outside of your normal personality, if you want. (it might instill Mufasa's lion courage in you).

And my work is apparently "post-internet" (i googled "post-internet", like the intern suggested, and i don't think the term appropriately describes my work).

3.

My Thoughts
(Charlie James)

Gallery name — Charlie James

Location — Chinatown, Los Angeles

Date — Thursday, May 8, 2014

Lasted time frame — Approximately fifteen minutes

Okay, similar process - different gallery. This time around i called before walking-in. Not because i wanted to make sure the curator was there, and not an intern. But because i got terribly lost and i needed directions... The location was a bit inconspicuous. When i called i simply acted as if i was someone who was eager to check out their current exhibition. i conveniently forgot to mention that i was an artist about to do an unsolicited artist submission by walking-in with his artwork. And, oh yeah, it was the director/owner who picked up the phone. Seems like i won't be dealing with a scared intern this time around...

As last time, people's eyes are gazing at me from all corners of the street. i guess i still look ridiculous carrying all these things with me. A curious one smiles. Goes, "is that a project you have in that mailing tube?" i pick up my eyes from wherever they were lingering and return his smile. i answer, "Yeah, it's a 40 x 40 hand painted print i'm about to show this gallery down the block." Grinning, he says, "Cool, good luck man!"

i take a deep breath, relieved, that i'm finally in front of the space. i'm greeted by a white building with black French doors. it has big square windows on each side with tons of sunlight flooding its interiors.

i can see the art hanging on the authoritative white gallery walls in there blinding glory. There's no one in site as i walk-in. All i hear is the sound of my footsteps pacing around the cement floors. i study the work of the current exhibiting artist as i continue to roam the space in my black oxford dress shoes. i think, "Seriously, who goes to gallery shows after opening night, it's so empty here!"

As soon as i finish this internal thought, i hear loud thumping down the stairs from a loft office space area. i return internally with amazement and go, "Wow..., i guess my mind, rambling, telepathically captured someone's attention! And they are here to challenge the statement i just made!!" i'm pretty thrilled by this mind feat i just preformed. in front of me is this six foot or so tall bald man with glasses. He is dressed in khaki pants and a pastel orange button down dress shirt. My thoughts scream, "There is life here after all! And i'm intimidated by his physical presence!" But this doesn't stop me. i walk up to him with all the confidence i can muster and say, "Hey!" - i shake his hand. Smile.

He catches me off-guard by asking, "Do i know you...? Where you in here earlier...? You look familiar." in my head i go, "Crap, he must recognize my voice from when i called earlier, asking for directions." i calmly respond, "This is my first time here."

Then with genuine enthusiasm i say, "i love the work that you guys exhibit here!" He reciprocates the enthusiasm i put into my last words and goes, "Thanks!" He then proceeds to tell me about the process of the exhibiting artist in the main room. Mentioning words like "spray paints canvases", "enlarges images of water droplets", "i-phone", and "new media".

i say, "Oh, cool. it's a complete transformation." He smiles at the fact that i understood what he just explained and goes, "Exactly." He then tells me there is more art in the back of the room and down stairs in the basement area.

i check out the rest of the art. The ones in the far end of the gallery, and the ones down in the basement. i enjoy what i see and honestly think i have a shot at exhibiting in the space.

i sway back, fourth, and around. My 4 x 48 white mailing tube and other belongings bouncing as i look at more images. i'm a bit surprised he didn't comment on the elephant in the room, meaning all the things i'm carrying with me. i don't think people usually carry all this stuff with them when they are checking out an exhibit. Maybe they do, it's just that i've never seen it before.

i walk back upstairs, and the space is still empty, aside from the art on the walls. i hear typing in the loft office space area. i think to myself, "it's time" - and boldly walk up the stairs leading to where the bald man with glasses is typing. i see him punching the keyboard keys of an iMac widescreen display approximately 21.5 inches'. it sits on a large table.

The office space area is riddled with tiny colorful gadgets and toys. They linger around as decoration. There are various bookshelves filled with art books. And the walls have art hanging on them. i break his concentration by saying, "The rest of the art i saw in the back of the room and down in the basement is equally as good as everything else." He swings his black swivel chair in my direction and says, "i'm glad you liked it."

With an inquisitive grin i say, "What's your selection process like?" He stares back at the soft glow of his computer screen.

Goes, "Whatever i like, i show." i then say, "i happen to have my work with me. Will you take a look? Maybe i could be considered for a group show?" He looks up from the computer screen. Says, "i'm busy. i'll give you my business card and you can email me. if i like what i see, we will be in contact. if not..." He shrugs his shoulders in order to non-verbally communicate the rest of his sentiments. i say, "Thanks." And he hands me his business card.

He looks me straight in my eyes and says, "What's your name?" i say, "Victor." He smiles. And reaches out to shake my hand. i shake his. Say, "Thank you for your time" - and walk out.

What i learned from this gallery visit.

Galleries still don't appreciate "unsolicited artists submissions".

When attempting a walk-in, you should have an idea of what you want to say. But realistically you have no idea what's going to happen when you enter the space. You might be confronted by an intern. You might be confronted by the director/curator, or you might just be confronted by the art hanging on the walls. Either way, leave room for spontaneity. Have fun with it. Live creatively.

This is an experiment. This is performance art. My main goal is to walk-in. See what happens and write a short story about it. Whether i get a show or not is not important. Be respectful even if you get rejected. Be understanding, if the person you're talking to doesn't want to take a look at your work.

if someone says they are too busy to look at your work, when you know they are not truly busy, say this, "if you don't like the images i show you in the next fifty seconds, i'll "thank you" and walk out."

Though the bald headed man with glasses made a kind effort by giving me his business card, the gallery was completely empty, aside from the two of us. if he could talk to me for as long as he did, he could have spared one minute to take a look at what i had to show him.

i suspect, looking isn't the reason they reject you though. i think it's because you're an unknown artist that just invaded their space. They assume that your just another person who wants to submit art that's probably not good. i can understand their assumption. i'm aware that we currently live in a time where everyone is making stuff. Where everyone is "something".

But i believe that there are some diamonds in the ruff. The issue is that it's getting harder for them to shine. Sure you can say the internet has made it easier for someone to get discovered, but it has also made it harder, because everyone is trying to get discovered. Everyone is sending emails. Everyone has a Facebook, instagram, and twitter account. Everyone wants you to check out his or her work. Everyone is raising hands and yelling, "look at me!"

4.

My Thoughts
(CB 1)

Gallery name — CB1

Location — Downtown, Los Angeles

Date — Saturday, May 17, 2014

Lasted time frame — Approximately eight minutes

All of this is a spontaneous experience. it's all up to chance. it's a game of reacting to people's reactions. For me, it's improv. For them, it's real life. They are unaware that i'm performing and that they are part of the performance. in a way, i'm exhibiting in their gallery even though they don't want me to. Even though they refuse to look at my art. They are looking at my art. And taking part in my art. And the gallery is a staged construction filled with props.

The rhythm of the city is in full bloom. it's loud and chaotic. i hear voices chattering as car stereos blast loud distorted radio hits into the smog-filled air. All around me, a seamless panoramic image of people walking with breathtaking swiftness. Clutching shopping bags, purses, and i-phones. Their summer skins slick with sweat. it feels a bit like New York, even though it's not. People are entering and exiting fabricated superstructures shooting up to the sky. in front of me. Block after block of brightly lit storefronts and window displays, stretching as far as the eye can see.

Where there's a short one - there's a tall one, where there's a fat one - there's a skinny one, where there's a symmetrical one - there's an A-symmetrical one. i weave in and out of the maze of people traffic. i'm trying to not poke anyone with my 4 x 48 white mailing tube.

i don't look as ridiculous as i usually do, even though i'm carrying all my usual things with me. it's the city, everyone looks interesting.

i spot CB1 as i continue to walk. it sits at the base of a towering off-white cement building. it has huge glass windows that allow you to see its contents from the outside. i pause slightly. Get rid of my fear and say to myself, "Here we go".

immediately i'm a bit nervous as i push the door open. There are four people standing and talking at the front desk area to my right. i'm nervous, because anyone of them could be the curator. Anyone of them could be the director/owner. Anyone one of them could be the intern. Anyone could be the assistant. Anyone could be anyone, and i don't know who is which.

Enthusiastically i say, "Hey!" Their responses are rather dull. Just head nods with no eye contact. i think, "Okay... this is going to be tuff." internally i decide, "Fine, just walk around. Check out the show. And come back to see who is still hanging around."

My feet pace the brown beat up cement floors of the gallery. i direct my attention on art hanging on the authoritative white gallery walls. i enjoy what i see. A piece in the middle of the room compels me to study it.

it's found Styrofoam that's been spray painted various colors and pieced together. it's a sculpture of sorts. in the corner of my eye, i see two people walk in. They scurry past the front desk and start looking at the exhibit. i think, "Wow, people do come out to exhibitions after opening night. Even if few."

i walk into another room filled with art. i see painted portraits on large canvasses. All of a sudden blaring sirens and horns penetrate the cement walls of the gallery and my ears.

i look out the huge glass windows to catch a glimpse of what's happening on the street. The scenery is a mess of police cars and fire trucks trying to maneuver through dense city traffic. i look back at the art and wait till the sirens fade.

i glance at the light Oakwood front desk area. The four men are still there. Conversing. i can't make out what they are saying. i just see mouths moving in turns. i recognize one of them now. The director. He is a bald man with black-rimmed glasses. He is wearing a colorful long-sleeved button down flannel shirt. His chin is covered with a gray and white beard. Honestly he looks like he could be the brother of the director/owner of the Charlie James Gallery i previously walked-in on. i think internally, "Maybe the bald man with glasses aesthetic is a fashion trend in the art world right now and i'm just now getting hip to it. Or maybe, every man that's a director/owner at a gallery is someone of old age who is losing both hair and eyesight."

i breath out deeply.

i bring to mind a quote from one of my favorite films, "Zombieland." i say to myself, "it's time to nut up or shut up." i walk up to the four men. Already there is tension. it's as if they know why i'm here. it's as if they know what i'm about to say. it's as if they were tipped off by a previous gallery i walked-in on.

i get straight to the point, wanting to end this scene in my life's movie as quick as possible. i look the director in the eye and say, "i enjoyed the exhibit, what's your selection process like?"

He is sitting down on a chair behind the desk, with an annoyed expression. He looks up at me. Then his eyes dart around the space. The three other heads briefly sway in my direction. The air is thick. The tension is a sharp blade threatening to stab me if i don't leave.

Finally, he answers in a stumble of words. They come out in the formation of something like, "We pick the artist's we like... Currently there is so and so represented by us. We also do group shows..."

i look at my 4 x 48 white mailing tube. i look at my faux leather messenger bag that's holding my 11 x 14 portfolio and aluminum prints. i say, "i happen to have my art with me. i know you guys don't like unsolicited artist submissions, but will you take a look?"

i'm performing. This is research. This is thrilling. i'm excited. i'm scared. The tension is so deep. So uncomfortable. So awkward. it's like asking the person you're in a relationship with why they want to break up with you. And they don't want to give you an honest answer.

By now, i know when someone is about to give me an excuse, and right now i feel like i'm about to receive one.

i refer to this feeling as my "gallery walk-ins Spidey-senses". it's an intuitive feeling that warns me of coming excuses or rejection of some sort. Similar to the super powers of Spiderman called "Spidey-sense", which is an intuitive feeling that warns him of coming danger. Anyway, my "gallery walk-ins Spidey-senses" are tingling.

The director/owner, who's bald and wearing black-rimmed glasses, still looks annoyed, and i know he's about to let out a reason why he can't look at my work. "Well, we actually have an appointment with someone else in a bit. You can drop by when we are less busy... maybe sometime during Wednesday through Friday."

internally i'm elated because my "gallery walk-ins Spidey-senses" didn't fail me and tingled right on cue! He said what i expected him to say. i look down at the director/owner, who's bald and wearing black-rimmed glasses, and say, "Can i make an appointment now?" He shifts uncomfortably in his chair.

Says, "it's better if you just drop by during one of those days." i say, "Okay, and thank you."

i walk out, and the city still looks like the city. An abundance of visual and auditory information screaming in your face. Luckily my car is safe and without a ticket. i hop in and quickly jot down notes on my i-phone of the experience so i don't forget the details. i drive home and drop off my art. Then i cruise to a "Barnes & Noble" and type out the short story you're currently reading.

Zombieland. Dir. Ruben Fleischer. By Rhett Reese and Paul Wernick. Perf. Jesse Eisenberg, Woody Harrelson, Emma Stone. Sony Pictures Home Entertainment, 2009. DVD

What i learned from this gallery visit.

Galleries still don't appreciate "unsolicited artists submissions".

i have built up a kind of super power. My "gallery walk-ins Spidey-senses" - an intuitive feeling that warns me of coming excuses or rejection of some sort. it's incredibly helpful.

The more established the gallery, the more uncomfortable their reaction is going to be towards you.

The reaction is usually communicated non-verbally. it's a facial expression and body language that says, "Do you know where you are…?" Who are you? Did you really just ask us to take a look at your portfolio? Did you really just ask us if you can exhibit here?" Regardless, be kind. Smile. And keep your composure. Live your life creatively.

This process becomes 100% harder, when other people are standing around you. You have to decide within minutes, what's going to work best for each situation. You never know what or whom you're going to encounter. There is uncertainty. There is the unknown. And the best way to deal with fear and all these other factors? Simply confront them. Simply, "nut up or shut up".

And though art is about breaking rules, they are like every other institution that sets up boundaries. They don't like it when you break or challenged their rules. Still, you must break down their walls, because that's the role of the artist.

But don't expect them to comply easily. There will be opposition.

My Thoughts
(Kohn Gallery)

5.

Gallery name — Kohn Gallery

Location — N Highland Ave, Los Angeles

Date — Saturday, May 24, 2014

Lasted time frame — Approximately fifteen minutes

i swerve my tiny red British car into the parking lot. it now sits perfectly between two white lines. i walk toward the entrance of an approximately 12,000 sq. ft. intimidating cement building with huge glass doors and windows. i keep thinking and feeling like the overcast weather currently hanging above me is an ominous sign that things are about to go terribly wrong. i get a little annoyed that my fear is generating these types of thoughts right now. i quickly remember that this is a performance and that i can become whatever character i want to be. i can be a confident one, if i think like a confident one. So i begin. Confidence starts surging through my brain. My body responds and i start walking, like a confident one. Everything about me radiates electric red confidence.

i'm carrying my usual props. 4 x 48 white mailing tube. 11 x 14 frosted green glass portfolio. One 8 x 10 aluminum metal print with a high gloss finish. One 8 x 10 aluminum metal print with a brushed matte finish. And two pairs of heavy white cotton gloves. i'm dressed a little better this time around.

i'm wearing a black V-neck wool sweater vest. it acts as a compliment to the blue oxford long sleeve button down shirt that's underneath it. i also have on a blue driver cap. Black-rimmed glasses and black oxford dress shoes. i look the part of a young professional artist that's possibly delivering artwork to the gallery.

i'm now a few feet away from the high-reaching glass door entrance. i see, what i presume to be, three friends walking out of the gallery as i'm walking-in. One cutie and two guys. A threesome of sorts. They eye me with curiosity as we all exchange polite smiles. We acknowledge each other's existences. One of the guys swings the weighty glass door open and holds it open until i completely walk-in. After i'm through, i turn back with a big smile, go, "Thanks!"

As they walk off into the distant parking lot i start to imagine what their internal thoughts about me might have sounded like if they were verbal. "Who was that guy…? He looked absolutely ridiculous carrying all that stuff with him to the gallery exhibit!" Or maybe they thought, "An artist delivering artwork to the space… Let's open the door for him!" Obviously, i have no clue what they were thinking. i can't read minds. Realistically they were just being kind people.

The swirl of chill air conditioning rises up and kisses my face. it's cold, but sweet. My eyes capture the approximately 22 ft. high ceiling space in a panoramic image. My thoughts are immediate and flooding with excitement. "This space is huge! Beautiful."

The art isn't hanging on the typical ubiquitous authoritative white gallery walls. instead, it's hanging on a pastel pink more welcoming authoritative gallery wall. And the art?

29

it amazes every fiber in my body and jolts a wide smile on my face.

There are a lot more people here than i anticipated. Approximately fifteen to twenty bodies. All roaming around, looking at the art, and taking pictures of the art pieces they like with their i-phones. And, of course, some are using the art as background imagery for their beloved instagram #selfies or #artselfies. i start maneuvering through the exhibit. Being extra careful about the way my 4 x 48 white mailing tube might swing.

i take my time studying the skill presented on the huge oil paintings in front of me. They range in sizes of 90 x 60, 66 x 42, 72 x 48, and other various proportions. Their frames are immaculate in their custom designs. The images themselves depict eccentric whimsical characters that exist in these dark fairy tale wonderlands. And each painting has its own unusual narrative that beckons you to unravel its mysteries. i start to realize that i've seen this person's work before. But where...Then it hits me. Tyler, The Creator's album cover for "WOLF." The artist is Mark Ryden! and this is his solo exhibition.

i walk circles around the rest of the show. i stand out. Mainly because i have all these things with me. i'm still thinking confident. Walking confident. i'm still acting as if i'm one of the galleries represented artist delivering artwork to the space.

i direct my gaze to the long white front desk area.

it's positioned toward the glass door entrance. i see the backs of about eight people. i assume they are asking questions about the show or something related to that matter. i make one more round around the show, hoping that the front desk area will be clear of traffic once i'm done.

i finish looking at the show for a second time. And again i peer to the long white wooden desk in the front. Yes, it's clear! i think, "Fantastic!" The traffic of people has deviated somewhere else. "it's time!" The only person standing there is a woman with black hair. She is keeping busy by wiping down the top surface of the white desk with a yellow rag of some kind.

i walk confidently up to her. Smile. Then loud and enthusiastically i disclose, "Hey! i'm Victor." i hold out my hand in order to shake hers. She returns my smile. Puts the yellow rag aside. Wipes her hand clean. Reaches out to shake mine. i counter, "Nice to meet you!" My eyes quickly dart to the white bookshelves behind her. An assortment of interesting looking art books of some sort.

i dive further into the performance.

"i love this exhibit! This is a solo show right?" She smiles. Goes, "Yeah, Mark Ryden!" i ask, "Do you guys have any group shows coming up or do you mostly do solo shows?" "We do a mix, it depends on the exhibit." Her demeanor gets a little uneasy, as i then ask, "What's your selection process like?" "Well... the curator, Samantha, decides that type of thing."

Her eyes blink agitatedly and she asks, "Are you an artist?"

i grin, "yes, i actually have my work right here if you don't mind taking a look?" My "gallery walk-in Spidey-senses" start tingling. She responds, "Samantha is currently in an appointment with someone. i can give you her business card. Email her. if she likes your work, she will respond." She reaches down. Grabs a card and puts it into my hands. i say, "Thanks, will do!"

i hold out my hand to shake hers. She sits up from her chair and meets my hand with her hand. With a ton of enthusiasm, she says, "Have a good day!" i say, "You too!" - and walk out the building. i walk back to my car and think, "What an intimidating. Easy. Thrilling fun experience."

What i learned from this gallery visit.

Galleries still don't appreciate "unsolicited artists submissions".

Fear is not your friend. Be confident. Smile. Don't be rude.

Even if they don't look at your work, it's a win-win situation. You win, because you actually had Mufasa's lion courage to walk-in their space and ask for a show. You win a second time, because you grow as a person for just putting yourself in that situation. And, most importantly, you broke their rule. And art is about breaking the rules.

Also, most likely the person you're speaking with will try to diffuse the situation with one of these tactics:

"We are busy."

"They are in an appointment."

"We are not currently looking for new artists."

"The gallery is booked until the universe stops expanding and life as we know it ceases to be."

"i'll give you a business card so you can email us."

While giving you a business card is a nice gesture, it's also a polite way of shooing you away and saying no. The chances of them responding to your email is slim. They receive artist inquiries all the time. Does it mean you shouldn't try? No. Please try. Anything is possible.

6.

My Thoughts
(Honor Fraser)

Gallery name — Honor Fraser

Location — S La Cienega Blvd, Los Angeles, CA

Date — Friday, May 30th, 2014

Lasted time frame — Approximately thirteen minutes

i'm in Culver City's Art District. The sidewalk scenery is lined with
an abundance of gallery spaces. My eyes bring into focus the
names on the buildings as i stroll past. They register and ring in
my head as Maloney Fine Art, LAXART, JK Gallery, and Walter
Maciel Gallery. i get a little excited, when i see that Honor Fraser
is within my sights only a few feet away. i walk up a couple of
stairs, push in the double glass doors, and i'm in.

i see a girl with black hair and a black dress sitting on a swivel
chair behind the white front desk area. She looks bored. The
space is completely empty, aside from the art hanging on the
authoritative white gallery walls, the girl, and me. i break the cold
silence of the room by warmly and enthusiastically saying, "Hey!"
She responds in a rather dull lackluster way by barely letting out,
"Hello..."

i walk into an octagonal shaped room filled with massive canvases. They are almost the size of the walls they are planted on. When i say massive, i mean gigantic. Gargantuan. They wrap around the whole room and are approximately 60 ft. long. i have to take a step back in order to study them. They make me feel microscopic. As if they are the ones looking at me and examining me. My feet move in circles around the room. My mind offers this description of the pieces — "narratives that depict African culture and customs in a somewhat obscure and thrilling way." i like it, it's powerful.

When i get to the end of the octagonal shaped room i realize that it doesn't lead to anywhere else in the gallery. it's a dead end space. its entrance is it's exit. in order for me to enter the other rooms filled with art, i have to walk back out and go past the front desk area where the girl is sitting. i'm still not ready for my conversation with her. i want to see the rest of the exhibit, before i proceed with my unsolicited artist submission. So, i somewhat speedily walk past her without making eye contact or saying anything as i enter the other room. She looked disinterested as i walked past anyway.

This room is similar to the previous one. The only difference is its shape. it has more of the huge canvasses from the artist that obscurely depicts African culture and customs. There is still no one else in sight. The space is empty. i pull out my i-phone, snap some pictures for references, and open up the notes App. i start taking notes of my experience so far for the short story i have to write later.

i punch in observations, such as "octagonal shaped room", "dull hello", and "empty."

i slide my i-phone back into my pocket. "it's time." My mind and body go into confident mode, and i walk up to the white wooden front desk area where the girl with black hair is sitting.

i begin.

Loud and enthusiastic, "Hi, i'm Victor!" i hold out my hand. She shakes it with a smile. "Those canvases are huge...!!" i belch out. She comes alive. Her face brightens some more, "i know right!" "What medium are they, acrylic maybe?" i ask. "No, oil", She responds. "Wow, i can't imagine how long they took to dry!" i say as she snickers.

i'm surprised at how charming i'm being right now. i have this sort of out of body experience where i'm in complete disbelief that i'm actually going through this right now. Real life me is not this charming. Real life me is a shy, awkward, weird introvert who stays at home working on creative projects and reading books. And occasionally watches "Star Trek: The Next Generation" marathons. The T.V. shows, i might add, not the steroids injected J.J. Abrams Hollywood blockbusters. They are too exciting for me. i'm not a "Trekkie" though, i'm just a fan who believes "Star Trek" should be a world philosophy and technological philosophy that humanity emulates.

i begin the process of truly talking about what i want to talk about. "This is a solo show right?" "Yep." "How long is it up for?" i ask. "Tomorrow is actually the last day." "Well, good thing i came today...", i dive deeper into the performance. "Do you guys normally have solo shows or group shows?"

She responds, "Well it depends..." i feel the intensity of her eyes. They are rolling over me in an attempt to ascertain why i'm here and why i'm asking these questions.

i then speak, "What's your selection process like?"

She blinks. "Um..., we pick what we like..." i grasp my 4 x 48 white mailing tube with both hands. i say, "i happen to have my art right here with me, will you take a look?"

My "gallery walk-ins Spidey-senses" start tingling. And as quick as lightning she thunders, "i'm sorry, we don't "accept unsolicited artist's submissions.""

i smile because of the perfect formation of her words, "i'm sorry, we don't "accept unsolicited artists submissions", as they jump out into the air and enter my ears. She proceeds, "Are you in school right now...?" "No, i graduated three years or so ago. i do gallery shows from time to time." She smiles, "Oh, great. i'm sure i'll see your stuff somewhere then."

She continues, "You should just go on our website and email us... i'm sure if we like it, we will respond." i say, "Great, do you have a business card with an email on it instead?" She fidgets around. "Um... let's see..." She fidgets around some more, looking for cards on her desk.

As she looks for a card to give me i reach into my faux leather messenger bag. i have a surprise for her. i slowly pull out a colorful six pack of 1.25 inch'custom buttons i printed. They are from a body of work i created titled, "Sex, Drugs, and Office Supplies." On the top left hand corner is a link to my instagram page. On the bottom left is a link to my website.

She stops moving around and says, "i have these basic ones here." She hands me the card, and i say, "Thanks." Then i say, "i know you guys don't accept unsolicited artist materials but, i want to give you a gift." She shoots a curious but kind glance in my direction. i hand the buttons to her. She looks. Studies it and smiles a wide smile. internally i'm feeling great because i just got her to look at my work.

i just got her to accept an unsolicited artist submission, even though a few minutes ago she thundered lightning saying, "i'm sorry, we don't "accept unsolicited artists submissions". She looks back up at me and says, "Thanks." i hold out my hand. She shakes it. She warmly lets out, "Have a good day!" i say, "You too!" — and walk out.

i walk past a couple other galleries. i see one that interests me. i just want to check out what they have in there. i push the door into LAXART. i have no plans to unsolicitedly show them my artwork. The art i see is appealing, but it has no connection with what i do. i walked into Honor Fraser, because i feel the work they exhibit has a connection with what i do. i did research before walking in there to unsolicitedly try to show them my work. i know that they represent one of my favorite artists, KAWS. i know that the director there is Angela Robbins. This is not a random process. All the spaces i decide to crash are conscious decisions. i don't think it's wise to try to show your work to a gallery you know nothing about. You should take a look at what type of art they show. Look at whom they represent. Then decide if you want to make contact with them.

What i learned from this gallery visit.

Galleries still don't appreciate "unsolicited artists submissions".

it seems my own project is having an effect on me. it's transforming me in a way i didn't expect it to. it's curing my fear of talking to strangers or just feeling uncomfortable around people in general. The me who walks into these spaces is extorted. The person sitting at his computer, planning and typing these short stories is introverted. Perhaps this book should be called "Conquering introversion: A Manifesto" or "Steps to Becoming Less introverted by Doing Extroverted Activities."

You have to be extra acute in your observational skills if you want to accurately describe the short story you will be writing. You have to pay attention to tiny details. Things like the mannerisms of the person you're in conversation with. You need to notice and remember what they are wearing. The hair color. The twitches in your face and their face. Your internal dialogue. The cement floors.

if someone doesn't introduce themselves to you when you walk-in. Doesn't smile. Doesn't greet you. Acts disinterested. Do the exact opposite. introduce yourself. Smile. Greet. Be interested.

The "are you in school?" question. First of all, i look really young. So young, that i seem as if i bathe in the fountain of youth every morning. The last register person who carded me, when i was buying beer, offered this insightful sentiment and foresight, "You will be carded "forever!" You look so young!" But that's beside the point i'm trying to make. The point is this. The mindset behind the age question comes from a place that thinks, "Only a young art student who is naive and unaware of the "unsolicited artists submissions" rule would try something like this."

i can understand that mindset but, its half-truth. While, i'm sure, some youngsters blindly ignore the rules and do whatever they want without sound judgment, not all are like that. And, in general, i argue that youngsters are just more willing to break the rules, because the world is still new to them. They still have "anything is possible" floating around in the center of their beings.

Maybe it's because they understand that reality is malleable. That they can shape it into whatever shape or form they want it to resemble. Whereas oldsters are more accustomed to following the rules and reality for them is a solidified shape. That mindset thinks that oldsters wouldn't dare try to unsolicitedly show us their work because "they know better…, they are aware of the rules…"

This book is not about ignoring the rules and trying to break them without sound judgment. i'm aware that you have to know the rules, before you can break them. Picasso said, "Learn the rules like a pro, so you can break them like an artist." Yes, you can break the rules like an artist, but the rules you're attempting to splinter don't have to be just limited to things such as compositions, colors, techniques, etc. it could simply be breaking the "don't walk into our gallery and unsolicitedly show us your artwork" rule.

You should question everything.

When attending art school, i was the student who wrote this statement when he didn't finish his critical thinking paper on eugenics: "The latter of this paper is written with invisible ink." My teacher responded, "it's transparent in its invisibility!" - after grading it. Well, i got a decent grade. And decide to share what i thought was a clever victory with my friend who sat behind me. A little mad, she belched out, "i can't believe you wrote that and got a decent grade, and i finished my paper when you didn't!"

\- \-

"A Quote by Pablo Picasso." Goodreads. Web. 29 Nov. 2014.
<https://www.goodreads.com/quotes/558213-learn-the-rules-like-a-pro-so-you-can-break>.

My Thoughts
(M + B)

7.

Gallery name — M + B

Location — N Almont Dr, Los Angeles, CA

Date — Saturday, June 7th 2014

Lasted time frame — Approximately five minutes

i'm making my way towards the entrance of M+B Gallery. A black cat emerges out of some green shrubbery to my right. This black cat looks me straight in my eye. it doesn't move, and neither do i. This black cat seems surprised to see me here. i share the same sentiment, because i'm equally surprised by its sudden manifestation. i look this black cat straight in its gray marbled eye. We have this "deer in the headlights" moment. Both of us are waiting and anticipating the other's next movement.

it lifts a paw from the ground. Takes another quick look at me and quickly dashes underneath the wooden black and white building to my left. i'm not the superstitious type, but the conditioned facts my mind has on black cats can't help but say, "Oh man... this is an ominous sign that this walk-in is going to go horrible!"

i'm a bit uneasy now, but i continue towards the entrance of the gallery. internally i think, "if this black cat and me could communicate, i would ask, "do you know you're an ominous sign to some people?" This black cat would probably respond, "No, i'm just a cat."

i encounter the ubiquitous, authoritative white gallery walls in there blinding glory as i enter the space. The work hanging is provocative in a sexual way. i spend some time studying the art and experiencing the dynamics of the space. i suddenly spot another room with a Jessica Eaton photograph. i get excited and walk towards the room, because i adore her work.

i see a girl wearing a black shirt. She has a two-tone hair color, mix of blond and black. She is sitting on a swivel chair by a desk. An iMac widescreen display that's approximately 21.5 inches' sits on it. i speak, asking, "is this the entire exhibition? is there anything else in this room?" She swivels her chair, faces me. Smiles. "That's the entire exhibition, this is our office space."

Then and there i decide to start the performance, even though i'm not completely ready. i want to look at more art, but there is no more art to look at. And she's already in front of me. i react to the situation. i laugh a little and say, "Oh..., okay."

i hold out my hand and warmly say, "i'm Victor!" She shakes it hesitantly. She acts like she doesn't know why i'm introducing myself and i feel her eyes trying to ascertain why i'm here. My eyes dart from the Jessica Eaton photograph on the wall to hers. i get straight to the point of the matter and the words, "Do you guys have any group shows coming up?" come out of me. She looks a bit uneasy. She responds, "Yes..., we have some coming up later in the summer."

i make my next move and say, "What's your selection process like?" She answers, "Well, we already have enough artists... and usually we pick who we like or it's by a gallery artist recommendation."

i then say, "i happen to have my work with me right here. Will you take a look?"

My "gallery walk-ins Spidey-senses" have been tingling off the radar since i had that encounter with the black cat, so i expect 100% rejection of some sort. She cringes a little. Mutters, "No... but you could email us." "Do you have a business card i can have?" i ask. She fidgets below her desk and hands me one. She then says, "You should stop by and check out one of our group shows to get an idea of what we show."

i grin slightly and say, "Sure, and even though you won't look at my work, i'd like to give you a gift anyway." i reach in my faux leather messenger bag to get my colorful six pack of 1.25 inch' custom buttons from my series "Sex, Drugs, and Office Supplies" to give to her.

i feel her gaze on me intensify. She's looking at me, as if i'm getting ready to throw red paint i don't have onto her white fur coat that she is not wearing. i pull out the six pack of custom buttons and hand it to her. She relaxes and smiles at me.

i hold out my hand and say, "Thanks for your time." And again she's a bit hesitant to shake my hand, but she eventually commits. i say, "Goodbye and have a good day!" i walk out the space thinking, "That was "uncomfortably sloppy, and quick."

Maybe the interaction i previously had with the black cat had an impact on me, even though i'm not the superstitious type. i also wonder what she will do with the gift i gave her. Set it aside and forget? Maybe pay attention to it? i don't know. What's important is that i placed it in her hands.

What i learned from this gallery visit.

Galleries still don't appreciate "unsolicited artists submissions".

Beware of black cats crossing your path, if you're superstitious! And if you're not don't let your conditioned irrational thoughts on black cats overtake you.

There's a 99% chance they will not look at your work even though you have it with you. Or, especially if you have it with you. instead give them a gift that's really your work in promotional form. it's pretty much a promo piece masquerading as a gift that you're handing in person instead of mailing.

And use the word "gift" because it brings a smile to everyone's face. Buttons. Postcards. T-shirts. Or get creative and inventive. Make something completely different.

They will be uneasy around you as soon as you start asking questions about showing in their gallery. Counter their unease with ease. Be polite. Be kind. Be respectful.

8.

My Thoughts

(ACME)

Gallery name — ACME

Location — Wilshire Blvd Los Angeles, CA

Date — Saturday, June 14th, 2014

Lasted time frame — Approximately 15min

i'm in front of this white blockish building with large frosted glass windows. i notice a black wall decal in a text that reads ACME. it pops against the glass as i try to peer into the insides of the gallery space. But all i can make out are fuzzy red and blue colors that i assume to be art.

i feel slightly uncomfortable as i walk-in. it's so quiet and empty. Each footstep i take seems to echo and bounce around the space. i study what appears to be a sculpture of sorts, installed on the authoritative white gallery walls. it's an assortment of materials. Painted plywood pieces. Blue, orange, and pink lamp. And a long tangled blue extension cord that's the power source of the lamp which is turned on and emitting a soft tungsten glow.

i continue viewing the art pieces in the space. The variety and diversity of what i see gives me the hint and indication that this is a group show. A pretty large one, too. Maybe fifteen or so artists. There are wall mounted video installations, various paintings, and sculptures.

One piece in particular catches my eye.

it's a yellow LCD screen mounted on the wall. it displays video of a man wearing a yellow and white checkered flannel long sleeve button down shirt. He is cutting out shapes into a wooden wall with a saw that he's grasping.

i walk around and finish looking at the rest of what the exhibit has to offer. The space remains empty. No one is currently looking at the art, except for me. The thought, "i could literally install my art on some free wall space and walk out..." pops into my head. With how empty the space is, i doubt anyone would immediately notice.

But if i decide to do that, it would have to be a "hang and run" situation. Similar to the "hang and run" "Banksy" pulled off when he secretly installed his artwork at New York's Metropolitan Museum of Art. His performance was skillfully beautiful and cat-like. i'm not sure i could pull off the quality of being "skillfully beautiful and cat-like." So, of course, i'm not going to attempt a "hang and run" here. Plus, sneaking into gallery exhibits (or in Banksy's case, classic museums) and secretly installing your artwork is not the theme of this book. Breaking the "don't walk into our gallery and unsolicitedly show us your artwork" rule is the theme of this book.

And i'm aware what i'm doing is a cute puppy, compared to what he did. instead of asking to be part of an exhibit, he took action and physically put himself in the exhibit.

i make my way towards the office space area of the gallery. i see a woman with black hair. She is sitting on a swivel chair facing an iMac widescreen display. Black pants, a blue shirt, with diamond decorations on her lapels dress, her body. She is focused intently on the computer screen. The details on there seem to be triggering her eager attention.

The office space area is far back from me so with warm enthusiasm i yell, "Hey!" to break her absorption and make my existence known to her. She swivels towards me. Smiles and yells back, "Hey!" There is a room filled with art that leads into the office space area, she is sitting in, via an open doorway. And the entrance to the room, filled with art, is halfway blocked with a white table.

She sits up and walks up to me. i ask, "is this room part of the exhibition?" She responds, "No, but you can take a look." i squeeze past the white table that functions like a barrier to the room. i study the paintings. There are few, but they are large and impressive. The woman with black hair returns to her computer. A small black and white dog runs up to me. Barks a little. Starts jumping around. She looks back to where i'm standing. Smiles and curiously asks the dog, "What are you doing...? You're crazy!" Her voice is warm and affectionate towards the dog.

i lean towards the doorway leading into the office space area where she is sitting on her swivel chair. i continue to ask questions, "This is a group show right?" "Yeah," she responds. "How often do you guys have them?"

She walks back up to me. "Um... we usually do solo shows, but we have group shows in the summer." Her dog is excitedly jumping around.

She is mildly paying attention to my questions and me. And her eyes keep darting back to her computer. Her body language and stance read, "i'm busy..., why are you asking these questions?"

i ask, "What's your selection process like?" She is about to say something, but the phone starts ringing. Her dog is still excitedly jumping around.

i politely say, "it's okay, answer it." As she runs back to the office space area she says, "Take a look at the folder on the table, you'll find a list of the artists in the group show there." She makes it back to the phone. Picks up on the second maybe third ring.

i take her advice and study the contents on the white table. There is a blue book with the title of "Art Fiction". And there is a folder that holds various documents. i flip through. i see a list of all the artists in the exhibition and the prices of their artworks. The numbers range from $28,000.00, $8,000.00, $4,000.00, to $600.

i pick my eyes from the folder on the table. i see an older man in a blue oxford long sleeve button down shirt. He is standing in the doorway leading to the office space area where the woman with black hair is still on the phone. i say, "Hey!" How's it going?" He smiles and says, "Pretty good." The man in the blue oxford long sleeve button down shirt sits next to the woman with black hair. She's no longer on the phone, and they start conversing about something. i squeeze past the white table again. i start studying the art in the room with the doorway that leads into the office space area.

in a way, i'm waiting for the woman with black hair to come back, so i can finish asking my questions. Two minutes goes by. Four minutes. i peer through the doorway and see that they are no longer in a conversation. They are sitting in their swivel chairs in front of a long wooden desk that stretches to the back of the room. Eyes gazing at the glow of their computer screens.

Seven minutes go by.

At this point, i'm aware that if i don't make contact with them, they will just conveniently forget that anyone is here. Still being polite, i walk into the doorway that leads into the office space area. i smile and calmly say, "i don't mean to intrude, my name is Victor." i hold out my hand and shake the man's hand. He smiles and tells me his name.

i then say, "i'm just wondering what your selection process is like for group shows?" He responds, "it depends on who's curating the show. Actually, this exhibit is curated by one of our artists." i ask, "So it's just based on whoever is curating the show?" He says, "Yes."

"Well, i happen to have my artwork with me right now. Will you take a look?" Already i know he is going to say "email us" or something along those lines because my "gallery walk-ins Spidey-senses" are tingling as usual. And my foresight doesn't disappoint me.

The man in the blue oxford long sleeve button down shirt says, "No, but you can email us your work." "Do you have a business card i can have?" i ask.

"Yeah, hold on a sec." He starts fidgeting around looking for a card to give me. Meanwhile i reach into my faux leather messenger bag and pull out one of my colorful six pack of 1.25 inch' custom buttons from my series "Sex, Drugs, and Office Supplies". He sits back up. Hands me a business card.

He is polite and tells me to email a particular email address. He says, "email to this one, all of us, we'll it that way." He then asks, "What's your name again?" i say, "Victor."

i then say, "Thanks! and i have a gift for you."

He smiles as i hand him what's really my work masquerading in gift form.

The man in the blue oxford long sleeve button down shirt smiles some more as i watch him carefully studying my work even though he just said he couldn't look at it. i say, "Have a good day, and thank you!" The woman with black hair swivels around to me. Smiles. i interpret it as ingenuine, but i smile back anyway. i walk outside, and it's another beautiful sunny Los Angeles day.

What i learned from this gallery visit.

Galleries still don't appreciate "unsolicited artists submissions".

People will ignore you. Be disinterested in what your saying and doing. Because A) They suspect you're ignorant of their rules, because your attempting to unsolicitedly show them your work. B) They don't know you. C) They might truly be busy and have work to do.

They will always give you a business card and refer you to their email address. Doing this is the best option for politely exiting them out of an unwanted situation. i dub it, "the pseudo business card trick". it's like when a girl gives you her number just to be polite. When in actuality she has no intention of communicating with you.

it usually plays out in three steps.

Step 1
They are going to give you a business card in order to escape an unwanted situation. (And that's if you ask for one, usually they just hope you walk out after they deny looking at your work).

Step 2
They will suggest that emailing them would be better because they don't want to reject you in person. it's safer behind a screen. it's like when someone is afraid to break up a relationship face to face. instead of breaking your heart in person, they do it over a text message or email.

Step 3

By the time you email them, they will probably have already forgotten about you. And your email will be lost within the vacuum of emails they receive from every other artist that wants to show in their gallery.

And the process of receiving an email back from them usually plays out like this:

A) You could get a rejection of some sort

B) You could get the defeating no response (Which always seems colder than the indifferent nature of the universe).

C) You could be one of only a few artists who acquire shows in this manner.

Still, be respectful. Smile. Live creatively.

9.

My Thoughts
(Shulamit Gallery)

Gallery name — Shulamit Gallery

Location — North Venice Blvd. Venice, CA

Date — Tuesday, May 22, 2014

Lasted time frame — Approximately 10min

So, i wasn't attempting to break the "don't walk into our gallery and unsolicitedly show us your art work" rule for this walk-in. This was an anomaly. An unusual somewhat spontaneous unexpected experience. it occurred two days before the "Kohn Gallery" walk-in, which was on May 24. i wasn't sure whether this short story would fit into this book or not, but with the way things unfurled i deem it necessary.

So there i was in Venice.

With the sole intention of relaxing and lingering on the beach, i wanted to do a bit of exploring and just enjoy the scenery with my older female cousin. i didn't have any of my artwork with me and i wasn't performing or planning on giving a performance.

i had no 4 x 48 white mailing tube that holds my 40 x 40 print on Moab Somerset Velvet Paper with deckled edges. No, 11 x 14 frosted green glass portfolio that holds various bodies of work printed on inkpress Luster Paper. No 8 x 10 aluminum metal print with a high gloss finish. No 8 x 10 aluminum metal print with a brushed matte finish. And no two pairs of heavy white cotton gloves.

This was my day off. My mind was tuned and set to radio station "relax and don't think about your work 93.5".

The concept of this book was a faded memory floating and melting away with the cool blowing breeze. The washed out hazy sunshine. The big chattering crowds of people slicked with sweat in their summer skins. The healing sound of the turquoise and bluish waves crashing onto the shore. And the sandy beach that seemed to stretch for infinity along the coastline.

There we were, my cousin and i, walking along, when her eyes had spotted this three story white, brown, and black modern townhouse looking building. She said, "Look, it's an art gallery!" pointing to text on a whiteboard that was attached to a black fence that surrounded the entrance of the building. it read Shulamit Gallery.

And like the cool encouraging family member she'd always been, she said, "Let's go inside and check it out!" She knew i was interested in this stuff. My face started twitching, while i cringed a little. The last thing i wanted to do at that moment was a gallery walk-in.

After all, i just done a walk-in two days ago. All i wanted to do was lay on the sandy beach. My mind was still fixed on radio station "relax and don't think about your work 93.5".

internally i thought, "it won't hurt to check out the show…" So responded, "Sure, lets go…" i was somewhat in awe of the space when we walked up to the entrance. The space was literally right next to the beach. And it had this super modern ultimate bachelor's pad atheistic. it was very stylish in its minimal design with big wide glass windows.

We had noticed that in order to get inside you had to dial in. So i punched in some numbers on silver buttons. A robotic beep. Beep. Beep, beep went off. A voice answered, greeting us, when i asked, "is the gallery open?" The voice had responded, "Yes," as the door had gone off in another beep... The door unlocked itself, and we walked inside the space.

The interior was typical. Ubiquitous authoritative white gallery walls in there blinding glory. We heard a warm kind, "Hello and welcome!" from the left side of the gallery. The owner of the warm voice was this beautiful woman with long black hair. She was sitting on a swivel chair behind a white desk. My cousin and i exchange smiles with her. We started checking out the exhibit when we noticed the space was empty, as far as people looking at the art aside from us.

We saw a mix of pen and ink drawings on paper along with sculptures. The pen and ink work's depicted obscure portraits of military men of power and whimsical deer with machine guns for feet. And the sculptures were the deer from the pen and ink drawings but in physical form. There was a black one and a white one, and both their feet were substituted with machine guns.

My cousin and i finished making our way through the exhibit. We went up to the receptionist desk where the beautiful woman with long black hair was sitting. She stood up, smiled and asked, "What did you guys think about the show?" "Great," my cousin said, "i liked the heavily armed deer with AK-47's for feet," i mentioned.

My cousin then uttered words that, at that moment, i didn't want her to utter. She asked the beautiful woman with long black hair, "When is your next exhibition?" And followed with, "My cousin, Victor, is an artist."

i cringed. Because all i' wanted to do was check out the show and head straight to the beach. My mind was still fixed on radio station "relax and don't think about your work 93.5". The last thing i' wanted to discuss, at that moment, was art.

The beautiful woman with long black hair responded, "Our shows are booked for the next two years, and we aren't expecting new artists anytime soon." My cousin who's always been lively and a friendly extrovert, belched out, "What! really?" "Yes, we do things in advance", the beautiful woman with long black hair had responded.

At that point, i was familiar with hearing statements like, "booked for two years" (or booked until the universe stops expanding and life as we know it ceases to be). So i wasn't surprised when her statements levitated in the air and entered my ears.

in fact, i remember my "gallery walk-ins Spidey-senses" didn't even tingle before the beautiful woman with long black hair said what she said, because they, too, were tuned to radio station "relax and don't think about your work 93.5".

The beautiful woman with long black hair then turned her gaze onto me and asked, "What kind of art do you do?" i smiled a little and said, "Photography that looks like paintings and illustrations." She then asked, "Do you currently do gallery shows?" i responded, "Yes, i've done a bit in the past. i actually have a group show coming up a couple of months from now."

She smiled. Looked me in my eye. And said, "i'm not promising anything, but take my business card. Email me your work. i'm curious to see what it looks like." i returned her smile and said, "Thanks, i'll definitely do that."

61

i pocketed her business card as my cousin said, "Goodbye and thanks" to the beautiful woman with long black hair.

We stepped outside the gallery and were pretty much on the beach. i turned to my cousin and said, "Good thing you spotted the gallery, i'm glad we went in to check it out." She'd smiled.

What i learned from this gallery visit.

Galleries still don't appreciate "unsolicited artists submissions".

Okay, so these are the main reasons i decided to add this short story.

1. Everything seemed to go pretty well even though it wasn't my typical walk-in. i didn't have any of my artwork with me. i wasn't performing. And i was with someone else. But it ended up with the same outcome as the others. A business card for me to pocket. But this time i didn't ask for the business card. it was given to me. And i didn't ask for someone to look at my work. Someone was curious enough to want to see my work. This short story is the anomaly. "The Twilight Zone" episode of this book, if you will. The unexpected twist. The "Michael Jackson" psychological thriller. Equipped with groovy dancing zombies of the midnight hour.

2. i got home and emailed the beautiful woman with long black hair. And guess what? (No i didn't get a show... and besides that's not the point of the book). But i got a response! And it was prompt, the next day...

Okay, so, every time a gallery has given me their business card and told me to email them, i did. Not days or weeks later, but the same night or following morning.

So far, i've emailed all the galleries on this list, and out of all of them, this is the only one that responded. So far at least... Maybe the others are busy. Maybe they didn't find my work compelling enough to respond.

Or maybe the email i sent them is lost in the void of other artist emails they receive all the time.

Either way, the rest of the galleries on this list gave me the defeating no response (Which always seems colder than the indifferent nature of the universe).

But this gallery gave me a rejection of sorts. Maybe not. i'll let you be the judge. This is a copy and paste record of our email interaction. This email record is not paraphrased. it's verbatim. i just took out her name for privacy purposes.

Sent email

Hey {%^&#$,

it's Victor.

i briefly spoke to you yesterday, when i was checking out the gallery with my cousin. Thanks for giving me the opportunity to share my work with you.

i attached some examples of various bodies of works, so you can get an idea of what i do. You can find each series in their entirety on my website along with artist statements, bio, press, and my exhibition history.

if you're interested in what you see, i would love the opportunity to make an appointment to show you these works in their physical presence. i feel, seeing things in person is usually more impactful.

Also, if you know of anyone else that might be interested in my work, i would appreciate it, if you could refer me.

Much thanks,

Victor k.

Website link

victorkphotography.com

Response

Hello Victor,

it was good meeting your cousin and you at the gallery yesterday.

Thank you for sharing the images of your work. i will keep it in our files and also will share them with our team, however as i mentioned, for the next two years the gallery is not excepting new artists.

We will keep in touch.

Best Regards,
{%^&#$

10.

My Thoughts

(Guy Hepner)

Gallery name — Guy Hepner

Location — N Robertson Blvd West Hollywood, CA

Date — Friday, August 8th, 2014

Lasted time frame — Approximately 7min

i pull out my i-phone. i'm walking to Guy Hepner. My caffeinated brain is firing neurons, thinking of what to say. i start documenting my thoughts as i punch the keyboard keys on the notes app. i'm thinking, looking. Typing. While simultaneously trying not to run into a person, stop sign, or other inanimate objects in my path.

i slip my i-phone back into my pocket. i pass the two story gloriously beaming Leica store. i get a little nostalgic and bring to mind the fond memory of the first time i went inside its immaculate interior a couple months back. i then pass the Beverly Robertson building with the Coffee Bean and Tea Leaf at the bottom. Loud chattering fills my ears from the crowd of people. All are sitting on the outside tables drinking coffee and conversing. My body swings right as i round the street corner. Guy Hepner is within my sight.

The August summer sun is beaming. Rays of sunshine flood the interior of Guy Hepner. i look through the gallery's huge wide glass windows.

The first piece i see is the ubiquitous Andy Warhol Campbell's condensed tomato soup can.

i can tell it's not a real Warhol though, because it looks more like an appropriation done by a contemporary artist.

The second piece i see through the wide glass window is a metal and chrome sculpture of a pink and silver bleeding dollar sign. in the moment, i internally think, "if there is a parallel universe that exist with me as a rapper, i would want the metal and chrome, pink and silver bleeding dollar sign sculpture as my rap necklace. it's so slick, pristine, and "gangsta chic" like Killa Cam's all pink aesthetic.

i push in the double glass doors. Welcome and embrace the chill air conditioning that tingles my body. A cute girl with brunette hair, glasses, and a black dress of sorts is sitting behind the front desk area. She pulls her eyes from an iMac widescreen display and says, "Hi!" i respond, "Hey!" My body swings to the right and i start checking out the exhibition.

immediately i'm impressed. i'm an instantly gratified person living in the instant gratification age. it seems to be a group show including paintings, photographs, and sculptures. The first piece that catches my attention is a 60 x 40 or so commercially whimsical photograph. it depicts a woman, playing tug of war with an alligator for an extravagant alligator textured blue purse. Both are biting the extravagant alligator textured blue purse, trying to pull it from the other. it's a Tyler Shields piece.

Next, i see a familiar piece that completely knocks me off my feet and makes my jaw drop.

i've never seen one in person before. i'm in awe. in complete disbelief that what i'm looking at is, in fact, what i'm looking at. i keep staring at this huge blue canvass.

i'm a little weak at the knees because this painting is…, a Basquiat! it fills me with joy. So i spend a moment. Or two. Or three. Visually digesting it.

After i'm done being a complete "Stan" of Basquiat, i walk to the back of the room and see the rest of the paintings there. i come across another artist who's work i adore. it's a Takashi Murakami! i've never seen his work in person before either. My excitement continues to escalate. Escaping through my pores. it's two of his cartoon/anime characters, named Mr. Dob. They resemble the famous Disney's Mickey Mouse character. One painting is a yellow version of the Mr. Dob character on a silver checkered Photoshop chess pattern background. And the other is a blue version of the character on the same silver checkered Photoshop chess pattern background.

There's no more art for me to look at, so i mentally start preparing for my unsolicited gallery walk-in. Though i haven't done a walk-in, in a while, all my motions and instincts remain intact.

i'm not nervous at all. But i still look ridiculous. i'm carrying my usual. My 4 x 48 white mailing tube that holds my 40 x 40 print on Moab Somerset Velvet Paper with deckled edges. My 11 x 14 frosted green glass portfolio. One 8 x 10 aluminum metal print with a high gloss finish. And two pairs of heavy white cotton gloves. i proceed to the front desk area of Guy Hepner.

it's "nut up or shut up" time. The words, "this is an amazing show, and is that a real Basquiat?" escape my mouth. i'm at the front desk area of Guy Hepner talking to the cute brunette with glasses. She looks up from the iMac widescreen display. Smiles at me. "No way! You don't own a real Basquiat and keep it in a gallery with a lot of sunlight hitting it!"

i laugh a little and say, "Yeah, it was hard for me to believe it was a real Basquiat when i first saw it." She laughs too. "it's an homage done by a contemporary artist," she responds.

"But the Takashi Murakami's in the back are real though, right?" i ask. "Yeah," the cute brunette with glasses says. i continue with my questions, "Do you guys mostly do group shows or solo shows?" "Group shows, we swap things out every day."

"Oh wow, what's your selection process like?" i ask, sounding surprised by the fact that they swap things out everyday. "Well, Guy buys everything. We own all the pieces." "Oh, so it's like his personal collection," i respond.

"Yep," the cute brunette with glasses lets out. "What are your prices like?" i ask. "Well, i sold the RETNA over there for seventy-five thousand." She points to a huge canvass piece covered with blue graffiti/hieroglyphics letters, as i look on with her. "And i sold a Warhol for twenty thousand not too long ago," she finishes.

intuitively i feel it's time to drop the verbal atomic bomb. i look into her eyes. She's extra cute up close. And 90% of me just wants to ask for her number. Or ask if she wants to grab lunch with me since the gallery is empty, except for her body and mine. But the minimal, though strong, 10% of me lets out, "i happen to have my work with me, will you take a look?"

As soon as i finish my sentence, the cute brunette with glasses speedily slips out her own verbal atomic bomb, "Seriously, i don't want to waste your time.

Guy doesn't listen to me. You can email him your work though. His email is #@$%@." i cut her off before she finishes telling me his email address. And ask, "Do you have a business card instead?" "Yeah, sure. This is his actual email, so he will see what you send him," the cute brunette with glasses says. She then hands me a business card that looks like a Visa black card.

i reach into my faux leather messenger bag. And pull out one of my colorful 6 pack of 1.25 inch' custom buttons from my series "Sex, Drugs, and Office Supplies". i say, "Thanks for the business card, this is a gift for you."

The eyes of the cute brunette with glasses light up as she studies and caresses the gift i just handed her. "Did you make these...?

Are these paintings...?" "Yes they are mine. i'm a photographer that thinks like a painter. i'm more inspired by painters than photographers. My work is more mixed media than photography," i respond. "Wow... these look like so-and-so's work." "Oh thanks, i'm not familiar with her work. is she a painter?" i ask. The cute brunette cringes a little and says, "No, she is an illustrator..." "Oh," i respond.

She then says, "Thanks for the gift!" i say, "you're welcome and have a good day!" The cute brunette with glasses says, "You too!" and i walk out as she waves goodbye.

i pull out my i-phone as soon as i'm outside the glass doors of Guy Hepner. i think, "This went pretty well even though i haven't done a walk-in, in a while." i then scroll through my thoughts like i scroll through Tumblr posts and start jotting notes of the experience i just had.

Zombieland. Dir. Ruben Fleischer. By Rhett Reese and Paul Wernick. Perf. Jesse Eisenberg, Woody Harrelson, Emma Stone. Sony Pictures Home Entertainment, 2009. DVD

What i learned from this gallery visit.

Galleries still don't appreciate "unsolicited artists submissions".

Attitudes change, when they realize your work isn't bad. Change, when they realize you're not a naive art student or artist who is unaware of their rules.

if you ask the person you're interacting with in the gallery to look at your work, they will find some way to say no. if you offer your work to them in gift/merchandise form they will say yes. Simply because the word gift triggers happy feelings in people. it's a present that you're giving that person. You're not asking them to do anything but accept a kind gesture.

And their attitude towards you will change if they like the gift you give them. All of a sudden they are asking you questions about your artwork, when earlier they just refused to look at it. They probably didn't want to look at your work earlier, because they wouldn't want to be in a situation were they were talked into looking at bad work. Once they see your work and realize it's good, they become curious. They start asking you questions. The tables turn. They become interested in you.

Being polite, instead of rude, makes the gallery walk-in run a lot more smoothly.

And, oh yeah. i'm pretty sure i had a better shot at getting the cute brunette with glasses number than getting a show at Guy Hepner.

So, to the person reading this book. i unintentionally ended up at Guy Hepner again. i want to briefly tell you what happened the second time around, because i feel it's somewhat relevant.

But in order to do that, we have to head to the future, specifically September 2014. And how are we going get to September 2014, you might be asking yourself? Time travel, of course, like the "Back to the Future" films. i'm Marty McFly, let's hop in my DeLorean and go "back to the future."

Ninth unsolicited gallery walk-in, (Section two)

Gallery name — Guy Hepner

Location — N Robertson Blvd West Hollywood, CA

Date — Monday, September 22, 2014

Lasted time frame — Approximately 10min

i tell my artist friend, who's visiting that a huge part of me doesn't want to go back to Guy Hepner, because i'm worried about someone recognizing me from the last time i did my walk-in there. He says not to worry too much, that he just wants to see the art they have, partly because he read the short story i wrote about the time i did my walk-in.

We walk into the gallery. it's flooding with light. Two guys are at the front desk area. And the same cute brunette girl i talked to during the walk-in i did last month is sitting on a swivel chair behind the front desk.

The two guys are holding papers. Conversing about something, while the cute brunette stares at the soft glow of an iMac display.

i walk over towards the middle of the gallery and start checking out a KAWS piece. it's a vinyl gray and white sculpture of his "Companion" character. i think, "amazing" - as i'm studying it.

"You're the guy who came in with the buttons...," a voice mentions out loud. it's the voice of the cute brunette and she is staring at me. Completely surprised i turn. Smile and let out, "Yeah, you remembered me...," i respond. The two guys that are holding papers and conversing stop and turn to meet my gaze. internally i'm freaking out, because this is exactly what i didn't want to happen, i didn't want to be recognized. The cute brunette catches me off guard and says, "Yeah, you made an impression." "Thanks!" i say still sizzling with surprise. "i just came in to see what new works you guys have up," i say. "Take a look around," she responds.

i walk to the back of the gallery where Akuna, my artist friend, is standing. i hear the cute brunette whisper to the two men standing by the front desk area. Her whisper sounds something along the lines of, "He came in here before, he is good..."

i find my artist friend at the back of the gallery. He looks up at me and whispers, "i was listening to your conversation, what happened?" i whisper back, "Oh the girl just recognized me from the walk-in i did last month, and apparently i made an impression..." Akuna smiles.

Responds, "Oh." i then turn to Akuna and say, "i think one of men standing at the front desk area is actually Guy Hepner, the owner of the gallery." Akuna shrugs a bit and says, "i don't think so..." i respond, "i'm pretty sure, i have a feeling about it."

Akuna and i walk back towards the front area of the gallery. i'm standing in front of a large Tyler Shields framed photograph depicting a female model's hand emptying a glass milk jar with an orange Hermes logo on it.

One of the men who was standing at the front desk area stands near me and looks at the photograph with me. 90% of me feels the man standing next to me is indeed Guy Hepner. Part of me wants to say something, but i resist the temptation. After a couple of minutes, the man exists the gallery as he looks back.

After he leaves, i walk up the cute brunette and ask, "That was Guy who was just in here right?" She says, "Yes, that was him." i then ask, "Would it be possible to set up an appointment?" The cute brunette responds, "No, he wouldn't like that." i then respond, "Okay, thanks anyway. "Bye!" "Bye," the cute brunette says as Akuna and i walk out of the gallery.

What i learned from this gallery visit.

Galleries still don't appreciate "unsolicited artists submissions".

i apparently made a good enough impression and was remembered in a positive light. i'm still not sure if i made a similar impression on the other galleries on this list. Maybe some remember me in a positive light. And others in a negative light. While some simply forgot me. i'm unsure.

When in the heat of a moment, what are you going to do? Guy Hepner was standing right next to me, and i resisted the urge to ask him for a meeting, yet alone say anything. Was that twinkling instance in time my "carpe diem" (seize the day) or "#YOLO" (You only live once) moment. Was i at the right place at the right time? Should i have seized the moment with my bare hands and molded it into what i wanted it to look like by asking Guy for meeting? i'm not sure, but i do know that this book is my "carpe diem" and "#YOLO" moment in a way. i'm seizing the day with my words in this book. And i'm living like i'm only going to live once, through the creative actions that are the manifestation of this book.

My Thoughts
(Gagosian Gallery)

11.

Gallery name — Gagosian Gallery

Location — North Camden Drive Beverly Hills, CA 90210

Date — Tuesday, October 7th, 2014

Lasted time frame — Approximately 15 min

This walk-in is going to be quick and terrifying. it's the last one, and i want to go out with a bang, not a whimper. if this were a video game, this would be the boss level. The final climactic stage where dramatic 8-Bit Nintendo synthesizer filled music plays aloud. And this boss is stronger or, in art world terms, (more established) than the previous galleries i walked-in on.

So, it's pretty much "nut up or shut up" time. And i intend to fully "nut up". My plan is to walk into the Gagosian in Beverly Hills and spit the most outlandish, magical, poetic jazz to them. Meaning, i sat down and thought of the most ridiculous shiny red thoughts to say to whomever i make contact with there.

This is the outlandish, magical, poetic jazz my shiny red thoughts composed.

"Hi, i'm Victor. Nice to meet you. i just came back from the frame shop with one of my art pieces. it's amazing! it's the collaboration Andy Warhol and Jackson Pollock wished they had created. Pop Art meets abstract expressionism. So can i have a solo exhibition here? Either in a month or whenever the scheduled is free?"

(They will respond to the craziness that just flew out of my mouth, and i will, in turn, respond with more craziness).

"i'm not sure Larry Gagosian will be happy when he finds out that you passed up the next Damien Hirst." (Then i'll walk out the door like a boss).

So, yeah, that's the outlandish, magical, poetic jazz i intend to recite aloud to whomever i make contact with at Gagosian. Maybe the statement is real, maybe it's satire. Maybe it's naive. Maybe it's living life creatively. i'm not sure. Or perhaps it's one of those things. Two of those things. All of those things or none of those things.

Either way, i've been memorizing it, bouncing it around the corners of my skull like a pinball in a pinball machine. And each time the poetry escapes my mouth i cringe with perspiring fear.

The panic, rational or irrational, screams, "You have to say this to someone! Not through an email or a text message but face to face! Are you ready for that?" Anxiety floods my body. i'm not ready. i get cold feet. My concerns are getting the best of me, and doing a good job of talking me out of this plan.

i'm worried because this walk-in is going to be different from the others. Different in what i'm saying and different in what i'm bringing with me.

i'm not bringing the usual list.

1. 4 x 48 white mailing tube that holds my 40 x 40 hand painted print on Moab Somerset Velvet Paper with deckled edges.

2. 11 x 14 frosted green glass portfolio that holds various bodies of work printed on inkpress Luster Paper.

3. One 8 x 10 aluminum metal print with a high gloss finish.

4. One 8 x 10 aluminum metal print with a brushed matte finish.

5. Two pairs of heavy white cotton gloves: A pair for me, and a pair for whoever is looking at my work. '

instead, i'm bringing the "Go big or go home" list:

1. My 43 x 43 modern white square framed artwork that holds my 40 x 40 hand painted print on Moab Somerset Velvet Paper with deckled edges.

2. A 10 ft. U-Haul moving truck. (For sheer ridiculousness and mostly because my framed piece wouldn't fit in my tiny red British car.)

3. My artist friend. (He's going to be filming the performance with my i-phone.)

4. My outlandish, magical, poetic jazz that i've been memorizing and reciting.

5. Courage that i borrowed from Mufasa in the Lion King.

Yes, fam, you read correctly. A 10 ft. U-Haul moving truck. i'm going to drive up and park it next to the yellow loading curb in front of the Gagosian in Beverly Hills. Then i'm going to "front" as if i'm delivering artwork to them... Will i get in trouble? Will they call security on me? Will they understand all my antics are just for a book/art project i'm attempting? i have no idea, but hopefully things don't escalate to that level.

it's currently October 6th, at night time. i'm pacing around my studio apartment, anxiety ridden, trying to decide if i'm going to go through with my plan or not. Everything at this point is nothing but ideas without action.

i haven't even ordered the U-Haul truck yet! i checked the site and saw that's it's available, but i'm too scared to commit to it! i'm terrified, but i can't give in, because in order for me to finish this book i have to complete this walk-in.

The issue is that i don't know if i should do the regular familiar walk-in like the previous galleries or "go big" with my outlandish, magical, poetic jazz and 10 ft. U-Haul moving truck. My heart is thumping heavily and i cave in. i can't go through with this. My fears get the best of me.

My artist friend, Akuna who's going to help film my performance is currently in my studio apartment. i tell him that i'm not going to "go big" tomorrow. That i'm just going to do the regular walk-in because i'm scared. Saying this doesn't make me happy. i feel deflated. A bit monochromatic.

Akuna gives me an encouraging pep talk about how the "go big" plan is a really good idea and that i should proceed with it. He says, "Who knows, Larry Gagosian or Damien Hirst might be there. And they might even give you an appointment because you have guts!"

Okay, so i doubt that either Larry or Damien will be there. Damien is probably chilling in one of his mansions. Sipping English tea and admiring one of his spot paintings with the biggest grin on his charming face. (Damien, in case you ever read this. invite me to one of your mansions. i'm a fan. Let's have tea.) While Larry, the "superman art dealer" is probably somewhere overseas dealing art.

Feeling a little better, i come to the conclusion that i want to go out with a bang and not a whimper. That it would be fun to do something i tremendously fear. That i have to confront it. That i would feel terrible and regret things if i don't "go big".

That i have to live life creatively.

That i have to break the "don't walk into our gallery and unsolicitedly show us your artwork" rule in the most fun and exciting way possible.

it's October 7th, 2014.

i'm both nervous and excited. i decided to go with the "go big" plan. i'm checking in at the U-Haul truck pick up site. Everything is good to go. it quickly dawns on me that this is the first time i've ever sat in the driver's seat of a truck this size. it feels like i'm holding the steering wheel of an 18 wheeler even though it's just a 10 ft. U-Haul moving truck. i spend around two minutes adjusting to the dynamics of the truck, since it's all new to me. As i turn knobs here and there i notice the imagination centers of my brain wishing that this truck was Optimus Prime, leader of the Autobots. So i could magically transform from an ordinary looking truck into an amped up super robot and save the endangered earth from the Decepticons.

My foot gently steps down on the gas pedal, and the 10 ft. orange and white U-Haul truck moves forward. i'm a bit off, at first, but i get the hang of it pretty quickly. i feel like a boss.

We head to my studio apartment and carefully load my 43 x 43 modern white square framed artwork that holds my 40 x 40 hand painted print on Moab Somerset Velvet Paper with deckled edges into the truck. i then quickly run through my "Go big or go home" checklist to make sure i'm fully prepared. Unsolicited artwork? Check. 10 ft. U-Haul truck? Check. Friend that's going to be filming with i-phone? Check. My outlandish, magical, poetic jazz memorized and ready to be recited aloud? Check. And the courage that i borrowed from Mufasa in the Lion King? Double Check.

i'm driving, and Akuna is in the passenger's seat. He is documenting the drive with my i-phone. Recording bits here and there, while asking me questions about the walk-in i'm about to do. We are approaching the commercial store front area in Beverly Hills. Stores like Fendi, Dolce & Gabbana, Gucci, Prada, and Saint Laurent line the streets.

The scenery is a kaleidoscope of desire's dancing and floating in a "wow" of spectacular. A lucid dream state of company logo's and advertisements. Where people are walking with breathtaking swiftness, clutching shopping bags, purses, and i-phones. Entering and exiting brightly lit stores while taking selfies.

We pull up to Gagosian and i park the 10 ft. U-Haul moving truck by the yellow loading curb like i originally intended. Akuna and i go over our individual plans together. This is our mission. And the atmosphere kind of feels like the action spy film "Mission impossible" with Tom cruise. Only we are art world spies. Here, to uncover the secrets of what happens when an artist tries to unsolicitedly show his work to an established art gallery.

Akuna's plan

Walk inside Gagosian eight minutes before me. Check out the current exhibition to make it seem like we aren't associated. Find a good filming spot. inconspicuously hit the record button when i walk-in. Then casually ask the person who witnessed my walk-in, what happened with that guy who just walked in with his artwork?

My plan

Wait till the clock countdowns seven minutes after Akuna leaves. Unload my 43 x 43 modern white square framed artwork that holds my 40 x 40 hand painted print on Moab Somerset Velvet Paper with deckled edges from the U-Haul truck. Unsolicitedly show my artwork to the person working at the front desk area as i spit my outlandish, magical, poetic jazz.

Akuna turns to me and says, "Be there at 3:15pm", as he opens the passenger's door and walks out. i'm in the truck, looking at the time the radio is projecting. i start reciting my manifesto. My declaration. My outlandish, magical, poetic jazz. i stop when i feel comfortable with how it sounds.

i close my eyes and hold my thoughts to the present moment.

inhaling and exhaling life. i feel completely alive. An ultimate rushing sensation. A brief moment of bliss. i open my eyes and a TMZ tour bus filled with tourist whizzes by. i look at the clock, and not much time has passed at all. i turn to my right, and my eyes study the white facade of Gagosian. The architecture of the building is quite stunning with its clear and frosted garage style glass windows. it also has this impressively huge single glass aluminum sliding door that's by the sidewalk. i assume it's to accommodate the more sizable artworks they receive. This is not my first time at Gagosian.

i was recently here, but just as someone who likes looking at art in gallery spaces. This time i'm on a mission, mission impossible. i'm not here to check out the exhibit for my performance is the exhibit. its just hidden within their exhibit.

My eyes dart back to the clock. it's time. Time to "nut up or shut up".

i exit the 10 ft. U-Haul truck and grab my 43 x 43 modern white square framed artwork that holds my 40 x 40 hand painted print on Moab Somerset Velvet Paper with deckled edges. i push open the glass door leading into the space.

immediately i'm thrown off. The front desk girl is not sitting where i expected her to be. She's a bit far from where i'm standing with my artwork. She's sitting on a black swivel chair.

Has black-rimmed glasses. Short hair that's a mixture of blond and black. And a white long sleeve button down shirt.

There are two extremely bored looking security guards in black suits further into the gallery space, which is flooding with washed out sunlight. They are guarding the art hanging on the authoritative white gallery walls. i think, they are eyeing me suspiciously, at least it seems that way from my perspective that's dripping with paranoia. My delusion flashes images of the two security guards in black suits tackling me. Pepper spraying me in the eyes as i cry out, "Don't pepper spray me bro! i need these eyes to create art!"

i cringe a little as i quickly dismiss my neuroses. My attention returns to the front desk girl with the short hair that's a mixture of blond and black. i start spitting my outlandish, magical, poetic jazz to her confidently, but calmly.

"Hi, i'm Victor. Nice to meet you."

The front desk girl swivels her black chair in my direction. Smiles. Says, "Hi!"

"i just came back from the frame shop with one of my art pieces. it's amazing!"

She smiles again. And in a sweet polite voice that sounds genuine goes, "i'm sure."

"it's the collaboration Andy Warhol and Jackson Pollock wished they had created. its pop art meets abstract expressionism. Will you take a look?" i ask.

She looks up at me with understanding eyes and lets out, "i'm sorry, its against our policy."

"Okay but, i'm not sure Larry Gagosian will be happy when he finds out that you passed up the next Damien Hirst."

She blinks. Smiles a little and says, "i know... i'm sorry... it's against our policy."

"Alright, thanks. Bye..."

"Bye!" the front desk girl with short hair that's a mixture of blond and black says as i walk out the gallery.

i point my eyes up and see my excitement is sky high climbing the stratosphere.

i'm elated that i actually went though with this. i truly feel that i'm living life to the fullest right now.

i carefully load my artwork in the 10 ft. U-Haul truck and sit in the driver's seat. i'm completely baffled by what just happened.

i can't believe that i just drove to the Gagosian in Beverly Hills in a 10 ft. U-Haul moving truck. Recited my outlandish, magical, poetic jazz and no one cared! i didn't go out with a bang! i went out with a whimper! i wasn't met with resentment. Security guards didn't tackle me and pepper spray me in my eyes. All i got was immense politeness! The front desk girl was so relaxed. Polite and sweet, that i felt it canceled out the ridiculousness i was saying to her.

My neurotic self had made such a huge deal out of this, and it ended up being one of the simplest interactions i've ever encountered. Ten minutes or so goes by, and Akuna walks out of Gagosian and enters the 10 ft. U-Haul truck.

He tells me that he talked to the front desk girl with short hair that's a mixture of blond and black. That she's polite. Beautiful. And wanted to ask her out on a date. When he asked her about what i was doing, that she responded, "He was trying to show his artwork to me." And when he asked her if what i did a bad thing to do, she responded, "No, it's just against policy."

i wonder what would have happened, if i told the front desk girl with short hair that's a mixture of blond and black, that i was completely aware that what i was doing is "against policy". That it's just that i wanted to see what would happen when i challenged that policy in person. Would that have changed anything? i'm not sure.

i also wonder if she told her co-workers about what happened? Or maybe my walk-in didn't even register as something significant to tell others about, because artists try stunts like this quite often.

Zombieland. Dir. Ruben Fleischer. By Rhett Reese and Paul Wernick. Perf. Jesse Eisenberg, Woody Harrelson, Emma Stone. Sony Pictures Home Entertainment, 2009. DVD

What i learned from this gallery visit.

Galleries still don't appreciate "unsolicited artists submissions".

You should confront what you're afraid of, because you might realize it wasn't that scary to begin with.

Driving a 10 ft. U-Haul moving truck for the first time made me feel like a boss!

There's a video documentation of my ridiculous antics taking place at the Gagosian in Beverly Hills.

Also, to the person reading this book, remember, when i told you at the beginning of this book that i would be refraining and omitting the use capital "I's" throughout this book, it's not because i'm ignorant of capitalization/grammar rules. it's simply because i enjoy the minimal architecture of lower case "i's" more than i do capital "I's." Well, this is how my lower case "i's" concept neatly fits into this book.

if someone who is educated on capitalization/grammar rules caught sight of my lower case i's they would immediately try to correct it. Their education on the rules would tell them to jump at my lower case "i's". Cross them out and replace them with capital "I's", as they did throughout my younger school years. But the problem is that i'm aware of the rules, it's just that i prefer this (i) sound architecture instead.

What i'm hinting at is that my lower case "i's" concept is similar to the gallery walk-ins. in the manner that both subjects are about being aware of the rules and still wielding the desire to break the rules. As soon as the person you're interacting with in the gallery figures out that your attempting to unsolicitedly show them your artwork and get a show, their education walls rises up.

They assume. They judge. They resent. Mostly because they have been taught and told to do so. Their schooling says things like these:

"Another young artist who is ignorant of our rules."

"Doesn't he know we don't accept unsolicitedly artist's submissions."

"if he were a sensible artist, he would be aware of our rules and know better than to try to unsolicitedly show us his work."

"if his artwork was any good, he wouldn't be asking us for a show."

Again, i'm aware of the rules. it's just that i thought art is about breaking and challenging the rules? isn't that what Duchamp did with the urinal? isn't that what Warhol did with everyday consumer objects? Didn't these artists and many others break one rule or another?

i'm not comparing my cute puppy antics of what i'm doing with the grandeur to what the aforementioned artists did. it's just that all of this is about raising questions and challenging something.

12

My Thoughts
(What i've Learned)

At the start of this adventure, i mentioned the idea of this book is to walk into ten hand-picked galleries that don't accept unsolicited artist submissions to see what would happen. That this is an experiment. This is performance art. My main goal is to walk-in, witness their responses, and write short stories about each individual experience. That the short stories will be a contemporary depiction of what it's like to be in the shoes of a twenty-something-year-old artist attempting to get a gallery to unsolicitedly look at his work.

That art is about breaking the rules, so why not break the "don't walk into our gallery and unsolicitedly show us your artwork" rule in a creative way?"

Well, i walked into those ten galleries. i attempted to break their "don't walk into our gallery and unsolicitedly show us your artwork" rule in a creative way. And you witnessed what happened via the short stories i shared with you.

Now, a part of me wonders what happened the moment after i left each gallery walk-in. Did the people i interacted with communicate to their co-workers about my intrusion? Did they say things, such as "an artist just walked in and attempted to submit his artwork a few minutes ago?". Was it even a big deal? Or did they simply dismiss the occasion? Casting it into forgetfulness, because artists walking into galleries, trying to get someone to look at their work and possibly take part in an exhibition, is a normal and frequent event? Where they intrigued by my presence at all?

i'm not sure.

But would they be surprised that the interaction they took part in was a prefabricated construction aimed at breaking and evaluating their "don't walk into our gallery and unsolicitedly try to show us your artwork" rule? That they were involved in a spectacle, that was being documented, and would later appear in a book of short stories? That even though they'd refused to look at my work, they were technically looking at my most current oeuvre and a vital part of it?

That even though i didn't exhibit in their gallery, i technically and theoretically exhibited in their gallery. it's just that i was in "Metal Gear Solid" stealth boy mode. Meaning, i was exhibiting in their space with disguised invisible artwork that didn't have to be hung up on the ubiquitous authoritative white gallery walls.

Since i theoretically took part in all the exhibitions they had, when i walked-in, my selected group shows exhibition list for 2014 would resemble something like this:

Selected Group Exhibitions

2014 October: Gallery Walk-ins (UNSOLiCiTED), Gagosian Gallery, Los Angeles, CA

2014 August: Gallery Walk-ins (UNSOLiCiTED), Guy Hepner, Los Angeles, CA

2014 May: Gallery Walk-ins (UNSOLiCiTED), Kohn Gallery, Los Angeles, CA

2014 May: Gallery Walk-ins (UNSOLiCiTED), Honor Fraser, Los Angeles, CA

2014 June: Gallery Walk-ins (UNSOLiCiTED), M+B, Los Angeles, CA

2014 May: Gallery Walk-ins (UNSOLiCiTED), Shulamit Gallery, Los Angeles, CA

2014 May: Gallery Walk-ins (UNSOLiCiTED), CB1, Los Angeles, CA

2014 June: Gallery Walk-ins (UNSOLiCiTED), ACME, Los Angeles, CA

2014 May: Gallery Walk-ins (UNSOLiCiTED), Charlie James, Los Angeles, CA

2014 May: Gallery Walk-ins (UNSOLiCiTED), Smart Objects, Los Angeles, CA

i'm aware, the experience i had during these gallery walk-ins doesn't necessarily paint the best picture of the art gallery world. But it's what i experienced. Whether good or bad, gallery spaces can be quite elitist and pretentious. Most likely than not, they won't even acknowledge your presence and existence with a "hi" or "hello", when you're checking out an exhibit in their space. They can be a tad boring and at times seem quieter than libraries. Traffic is low after opening night, and they tend to lack interest in the general public that doesn't have pockets deep enough to buy the art. The general public that's usually just thrilled by art.

And though art is about breaking rules. They are like every other institution that sets up boundaries. They don't like it when you break or challenged their rules. Are all galleries like this? Of course not, but a lot are. Do i hate the art gallery world? Nope, i would be a hypocrite if i did because i have exhibited in some of them and frequent their spaces for inspiration. i just feel they can push more boundaries. Let magical art unicorns run loose in their spaces without supervision and perhaps show some "TLC," (Tender, Loving, Care) to people checking out their exhibits.

But when it comes to unsolicitedly showing them your work, i can sympathize with their point of view. Mainly because no one wants to receive something they don't want or know what to do with. No one wants to be asked a question they don't want to answer. No one wants to be put into a situation they don't want to be in.

The forced approach of an unsolicited gallery walk-in is obviously not the wisest way to get galleries to pay attention to you. it's like trying to get a girl's number and she has no interest in you.

Let says you build up the confidence to go converse with a girl you don't know, but think is cute. You want her number, in order to get to know this individual more. You find her interesting and appealing in some fashion.

You catch her off guard because you're a stranger to her. She doesn't know you. it doesn't matter, whether you're charming or not. it's against her rules. She doesn't like your approach. She is the type of cutie that doesn't appreciate "random guys hitting on her". She doesn't want your phone number and doesn't want to go on a date with you.

And in that very instant you're chatting her up, she is sizing you up. Annoyed. And already has her preconceived notions about you. Her preconceived notions could sound something like this: ("Desperate random guy who has no chance with me. i don't want to give him my number, he's just wasting his time hitting on me.")

And the art gallery world preconceived notions would translate into something that sounds like this: ("Naive ignorant young art student doesn't know who he's talking to or where he is. if he's artwork was any good, he wouldn't be trying to unsolicitedly show us his artwork.")

The cutie (or the art gallery) could be terribly right! about her preconceived notions about you or, she could be astronomically wrong!!

Her ideas are just guesswork. Conjecture. Anyway, you get to the point where you ask, "What's your number? Let's go on a date." The art world translation being, ("What's your email address? Let's set up an appointment.") And the earth stops spinning round and around. Again and again. And both of you become a frozen moment in time.

She has two options for dealing with unwanted situations such as this encounter.

Option 1
The polite "i don't want to break his little heart" option.

She is going to give you a phone number. it might be a fake number that doesn't work. Or it might be her actual number, but she has no intention of remembering who you are or responding.

You will hit her up with a text at some point. Wait seconds. Minutes. Hours. Days. Weeks. And get nothing back. You might try to convince yourself that, just maybe, she didn't receive your text message or call. That there is some technological malfunction at hand. But realistically there is no technological malfunction, she just wasn't interested. Experiencing this "no response" is not always easy. But how can experiencing (the cold indifferent nature of the universe) which is the "no response" be easy?

Usually, the Antarctica like temperatures of the cold indifferent nature of the universe leaves you feeling like you need to drink hot chocolate. Feeling like you need to get a hug from a Godzilla sized fluffy teddy bear.

Feeling like you need to watch Saturday morning cartoons from the 90's. On the couch, with a cozy blanket draped over you, while a bowl filled with sugary cereal rests on your lap.

Leaves you feeling like you need to counterbalance its coldness, by doing or communicating something warm.

Anyway, this is similar to what happens when a gallery gives you a business card during a walk-in.

They give you their card in order to get them out of the unwanted situation of an unsolicited artists submission. You can hit them up with an email at some point, but you might not get a response. i'm not saying it's impossible to get a response. i'm just saying chances are slim.

Option 2
The straight forward "i have a boyfriend" option.

This is pretty much when she's being straight up with you... (Even though technically this could be another escape route for her.) She will look you in the eyes or avert eye contact and say, "i don't like random guys hitting on me... i have a boyfriend." in art gallery world this statement translates to ("We don't accept unsolicited artist submissions. We have enough represented artists.") At this point you just got to be a kind understanding gentleman. Walk away and brush your shoulders off. Play Jay Z's "99 Problems". And accept that fact that the art gallery world is a cutie that doesn't want to go out with you.

in other avenues, it seems this project had an unexpected effect on me. it transformed me in a way i didn't intend it to. it slightly cured my fear of talking to strangers and just feeling uncomfortable around people in general. The me who walked into these spaces was mostly extroverted. The person sitting at his computer, planning this book and typing this sentence right now, is less introverted thanks to this experience. Perhaps this book isn't about breaking the "don't walk into our gallery and unsolicitedly show us your artwork" rule.

i'm in my studio apartment in LA. i'm sitting on my chair that i like to refer to as my "throne". Warm tones of orange, red, and yellow light flood through my windows, courtesy of the setting sun outside.

i'm sitting. Thinking. Contemplating that maybe, the true nature and premise of this book is about concurring personal fear. Purposely placing myself in uncomfortable situations in order to become comfortable and grow from them. "Nutting up or shutting up." Stepping away from your Facebook, instagram, Tumblr, and Netflix accounts for like an hour, to live life creatively.

Or perhaps this book is hybrid of concurring fear, overcoming personal boundaries, while breaking the "don't walk into our gallery and unsolicitedly show us your artwork" rule.

Either way, the experience and process of writing this book has been enjoyable for three reasons.

Reason 1
i had conceived the idea for this book and started writing it the first year i moved to LA. Just another starry-eyed twenty-something-year-old, creative, moving to a major city to chase his wildest dreams. Trying to "make it".

i'm ending up writing the book i wanted to read.

A book that responds to the time i'm living in. A book by a twenty-something-year-old artist for other twenty-something-year-old artists trying to make it in the creative world.

individuals that are fighting against the pressures of adulthood, responsibilities, and college student loan payments.

They still have dreams of making it in the art world or a creative industry one day, constantly striving for time and energy to work on their creative projects. Trying to avoid living a life where you get off work.

Come home. Eat. Sleep. Wake up. Go to work. Repeat. And incrementally watch your dreams fade away bit by bit.

Artist's and creatives that are starting from the bottom.

Not the bottom of the rap game, like Drake suggested in his uplifting and rousing anthemic song, but rather starting from the bottom of the creative ladder.

Reason 2

Walking into these galleries reminded me of my glory days in high school as a skateboarder. it nostalgically placed me in a reverie of my rebellious teenage years.

Whizzing and curving through the asphalt jungles with an army of friends. Skateboarding in places where they clearly had "no skateboarding signs." And usually being chased offed or kicked out of these spots by security or some form of authority.

i don't skateboard as much as i use to, but the culture still pumps with my beating heart. Whispering to me always, "Stay anti-authority! Skate where they tell you not to skate, challenge and question your surroundings, always!"

This whisper is very much a part of this book and a part of the art i create. This whisper is a fragment of why i wrote this book. it's important for me to challenge and question my surroundings. Especially the way things work in the art world, when it comes to new young artists trying to open up doors. Or the way things work generally, when it comes to new young creatives trying to make it in any creative industry.

Reason 3

Before i could write a gallery walk-ins short story, i had to go into the physical world and put my ideas into action. i had to get my brain to move my body into each gallery, in order to experience something new. With our generation, things tend to happen at a click of the mouse and a swipe on a screen. if this book were a bunch of short stories about how i sat at my computer and sent emails to these galleries, it would be lacking.

Don't get me wrong, computers are dope, but the physical world still exists. Go out and play.

Even though i have a conspiracy theory that it's slowly disappearing, and "Tron world" is fast approaching, thanks to speeding technological advances. i have a belief that Steve Jobs isn't dead, he is just in "Tron" (the awesome 1982 science fiction film about computer software programming) getting the system "Apple ready" for the rest of humanity. i predict with my illuminati third eye that, one day, our collective i-phones will simultaneously start vibrating violently.

Emitting interstellar light while they rapidly feed off each others energy. Creating a massive vortex that will consume and suck everything and everyone into "Tron" where Steve Jobs will be waiting to greet everyone into a new technological apple dominated universe.

Also, i'm aware that there's a reaction for every action. This book is an action and there may be a reaction towards it. The reaction could be straight to DVD. Or it could be instant cult classic.

Or i may receive some punishment of sorts. if that's the case, the punishment would have to be similar to the task Principle Skinner made Bart Simpson labor over in The Simpsons cartoon. Me, being forced into detention. Walking up the chalkboard and repeatedly writing, "i will not walk into a gallery and attempt to unsolicitedly show them my artwork, when i'm fully aware that they don't accept unsolicited artist submissions." Over and over again, until the school bell rings. And i blast through the authoritative school doors, skateboarding into the scenic suburban distance.

And lastly.

Has anyone who's ever done a gallery walk-in, documented the process of what it's like and released it as a body of work? And does this book fit under the Craig Damrauer painting equation that asserts, "Modern art = i could do that + Yeah, but you didn't"? i'm not entirely sure, but i am sure of the statement below.

Galleries still don't appreciate "unsolicited artists submissions".

13

My Thoughts
(So, Who Am i)

So, who am i?

Alright, let's play the who am i game? Am i A, B, C, or D?

A) A new emerging artist who wants to live life creatively that happens to be twenty-something;

B) A photographer, that thinks like a painter, based in Los Angeles. Whose work aims to find the beauty in everyday recognizable objects, and whose work is mixed media photography that utilizes elements of photography, illustrations, and paintings.

C) A skateboarder turned photographer, turned laptop musician, turned writer, turned artists who wants to keep transforming;

D) A creative multi-hyphenate named Victor k.

Well, i'm all those things and none of those things. i'm simply someone who wants to create whatever he wants to create. A multi-hyphenate that operates, samples and dabbles in more than one creative industry.

To me this book is just another project in line of my previous ambitions. And though it's a written project, it still wields the contemporary pop art aesthetic of my visual bodies of work. This book is pop art, and i'm a pop artist. But my following project could be a sculpture. it could be an installation.

it could be a film. it could be a music album. it could be visual imagery like my previous bodies of work. it could be anything, as long as i find it compelling. i just happened to turn into a writer for this project. And it's not like i've never written before, i got plenty of practice writing bad middle school poetry for girls who didn't like guys writing them poetry.

Generally, if the public at large knows you for one thing, that's all they want to know you for. What they are doing is constricting and killing the expansion of creativity. Stopping creative individuals from being creative individuals through limitation. Telling them that they are only capable of contributing to one type of creative industry.

When a writer writes a book, they expect him to keep writing more books. When a musician comes out with an album, they expect him to keep coming out with more albums. When an actor stars in a film, they expect him to keep staring in more films.

Why can't an actor star in a film one year and come out with a music album the next year? Why can't a writer come out with a book one year and come out with a fashion line the next year? if the work is compelling, why should it matter? What are you supposed to do when you're a painter and you get a great idea for something outside of painting, like a fashion line?

Do you just let the idea slip by you, because of your inhibitions and lack of knowledge of a new subject? Or do you find the appropriate people to collaborate with to bring that idea to fruition?

Or, maybe, you've been painting and doing fashion most of your life so accomplishing a fashion line isn't too much of a stretch?

Just because Kanye West is seen as a rapper, songwriter, record producer, and a celebrity, doesn't mean he can't be a rock star creative genius who designs products and comes out with fashion lines.

Just because Aubrey "Drake" Graham started out as Jimi on Degrassi: The Next Generation, doesn't mean he can't be a rapper, singer, songwriter, founder of a record label, and founder of a clothing line.

Just because Pharrell is seen as a record producer and singer-songwriter, doesn't mean he can't be a fashion icon, designer of products, and someone who collaborates with dope artists.

Just because Donald Glover is seen as a writer, actor, and comedian, doesn't mean he can't make rap albums as Childish Gambino.

Just because James Franco is seen as an actor and celebrity doesn't mean he can't be an author, teacher, and artist.

Just because Tyler, The Creator is seen as a rapper and record producer, doesn't mean he can't come out with clothing lines and direct films.

Just because someone is known for one thing, doesn't mean they can't venture into new territories.

As a whole, i feel, culture should embrace more of this flowering of creativity in various industrious, rather than stigmatize it. Creatives shouldn't be limited to their creative industry boxes. Because though the box is creative, it's still a box.

So, who am i? Someone that enjoys anything minimal, whimsical, witty, and fun. Someone that has an affinity for everyday objects, skateboarding, music, and Woody Allen films. Someone who doesn't want his creativity to be constricted. Someone who wants to create whatever he wants to create. A multi-hyphenate that operates, samples and dabbles in more than one creative industry.

14.

My Thoughts
(My Work)

My Work

So iv'e decided to write descriptions of my work in two different ways to keep things interesting. One will be a typical description of my work, while the other will be an untypical description of my work. This translates into art world terms as, ("A conditioned artist statement and an unconditioned artist statement".)

it's a boxing match. We are in the ring. And the house is packed full with hundreds of electrified bodies. Screaming at the top of their lungs.

On one side of the corner, we have opponent one. A typical description of my work, or in art world terms, ("The conditioned artist statement".) This is usually the type of description or statement people expect and encourage you write. On the other side of the corner, we have opponent two. An untypical description of my work, or in art world terms, ("The unconditioned artist statement".) This is usually the type of description or statement people won't expect you to write. And will definitely not encourage you to compose in most circumstances.

They touch gloves and its uproar! pandemonium breaks loose.

Also, to the person reading this book. This is the black and white version of my book. if you want to see my works in their original colorful pop art form, head to my website.

www.victorkphotography.com

**The conditioned artist statement VS. The unconditioned
artist statement**

"Sex, Drugs, and Office Supplies"

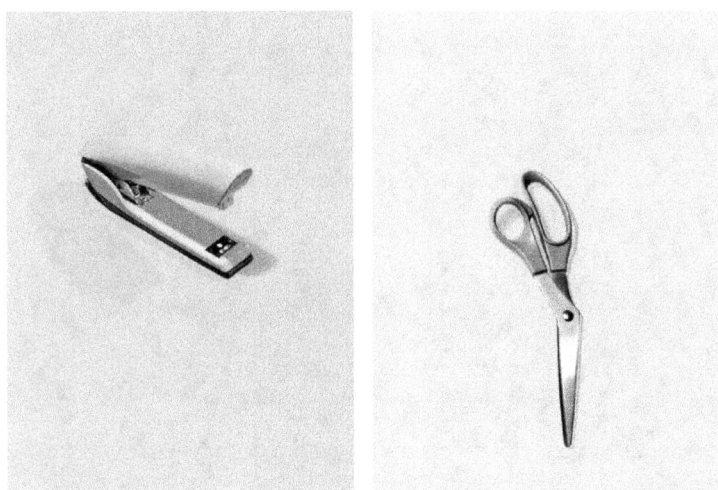

Typical conditioned artist statement

Sex, Drugs, and Office Supplies is a series that explores the
common perception and function of everyday objects. My
intention is to transform these objects beyond their banality into
objects of desire that encourage you to think of them in new
ways.

The conditioned artist statement VS. The unconditioned artist statement

"Sex, Drugs, and Office Supplies"

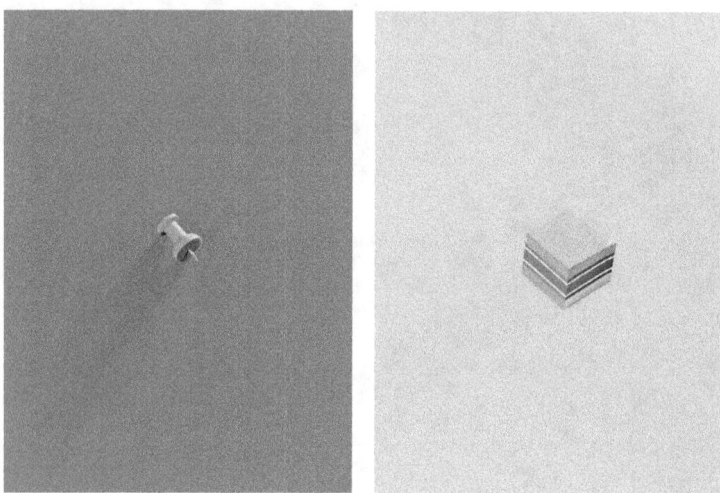

Untypical unconditioned artist statement

Sex, Drugs, and Office Supplies is an attractive girl you can't take your eyes off. She is a sexy, striking, vivid sensation that commands attention. She may not have much in her head, but the honest fact is that you can't tear your gaze away from her. Her beauty is compelling. She looks so good, it hurts. Hanging up there on that ubiquitous white authoritative gallery wall.

The conditioned artist statement VS. The unconditioned artist statement

"Sex, Drugs, and Office Supplies Buttons"

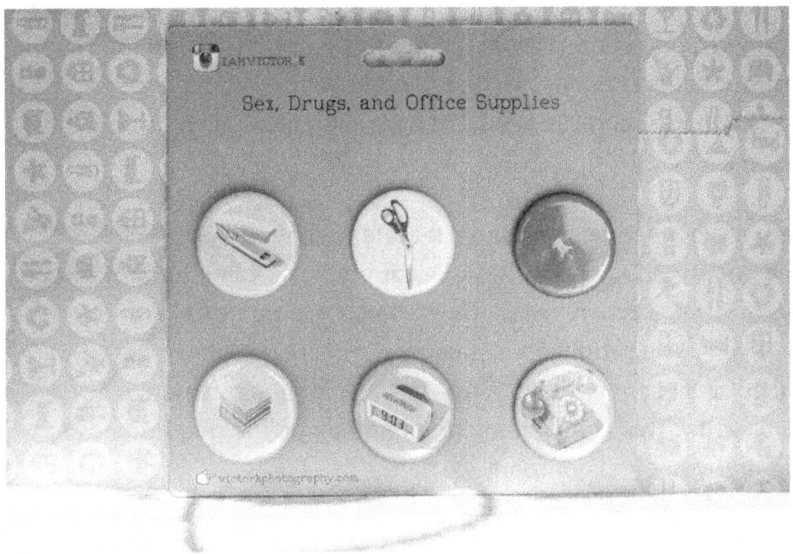

The colorful six pack of 1.25 inch' custom buttons i handed out as gifts when i did my walk-ins.

So it was a dirty, but good even fight. And the judges can't decide the Victor of the match. it's up to you, the reader who is currently reading this book to decide which statement he or she prefers. it's either the typical description or in art world terms, ("The conditioned artist statement".) Or the untypical description, in art world terms ("The unconditioned artist statement".)

Either way, one statement will probably be good Chinese food that you digest properly. While the other will be not so good Chinese food that gives you food poisoning and elicits puking motions.

There are consequences for each statement though. The typical conditioned artist statement will elicit praise or some form of reward. The glory you receive is because you put forth a "desired response". You produced a statement or action that seems conceptually sound, that the art world shaped and conditioned you to write. This is the statement that may be the good Chinese food that you digest properly.

The untypical unconditioned artist statement will be met with some sort of disapproval. Because it's viewed as an "undesired response". A statement or action that seems conceptually unsound, that the art world didn't shape or condition you to write. This is the statement that may be the not so good Chinese food that gives you food poisoning and elicits puking motions.

The issue is that most people don't want to question the establishment they are in. They tend to be afraid of bearing unpopular opinions that will make others glare at them with massive angry Bugs Bunny popped-out cartoon eyes. They don't want to be disliked. They want to fit in. it's safer to possess a crowd mentality and follow the ideologies of the group, instead of thinking for yourself.

it's more safe to produce a statement that will be good Chinese food that people digest properly. And less safe to produce a statement that will be not so good Chinese food that gives people food poisoning and elicits puking motions.

Let's have another boxing match. This time with an installation piece i want to bring to fruition in the future.

The conditioned artist statement VS. The unconditioned artist statement

"The mirror of inflated ego's"

The Mirror of inflated Ego's

Typical conditioned artist statement

This installation piece is a giant full-length square cubed mirror that reflects a bigger 15 ft. version of yourself, towering over you. its main purpose is to encourage people to believe in themselves more. To inspire viewers to build self-esteem. To instill that they can be as big as they want to be in life, if they choose to see their reflections in a new light.

The conditioned artist statement VS. The unconditioned artist statement

"The mirror of inflated ego's"

The Mirror of inflated Ego's

533K

SELFIE

YOU
(Looking into mirror)

15ft

SWAG

Untypical unconditioned artist statement

This installation piece is a giant full-length square cubed mirror that reflects a bigger 15 ft. version of yourself, towering over you. its main purpose is to make you stop, look, linger, and think to yourself: "You know what?" "i'm a boss! i'm Rick Ross. i'm DJ Khaled. "All i do is win." "Another one." i'm Drake, "i'm on one!" "i'm going to put a ding in the universe." i'm Steve Jobs. i'm a creative genius. i'm Kanye West. "i'am a god! Hurry up with my damn croissants!"

The mirror of inflated ego's is on my "grand ideas" top five list. These are ideas that i day dream about bringing to fruition one day. ideas that require a team of highly caffeinated creative shiny brains that want to make super dope art pieces.

Again, one statement will sit well with you, while the other may offend you. it's all about how you interpret my written words.

As your eyes scan these sentences, your brain will make robotic sounds, trying to process the information. After the information, digestion contemplation process. it will offer you an opinion of what you've just read. That opinion may be in favor of the information you've gathered, or it might not be in favor of the information you've gathered.

This is the last boxing match... This time with my series "A Beautiful Mess".

"DJ Khaled." AZQuotes.com. Wind and Fly LTD, 2015. 19 December 2015.
http://www.azquotes.com/quote/862320

"30 Hilarious & Inspirational DJ Khaled Quotes." Quotesforbros. Quotesforbros,
17 Dec. 2015. Web. 19 Dec. 2015. <http://www.quotesforbros.com/30-hilarious-
inspirational-dj-khaled-quotes/>.

"Steve Jobs." BrainyQuote.com. Xplore Inc, 2015. 16 June 2015.
http://www.brainyquote.com/quotes/quotes/s/stevejobs100189.html

West, Kanye. I'am a god. Hurry up with my damn croissants. "I'Am a God." Yeezus.
Youtube video. Def Jam. 2013. Rap Genius.18 June 2015. http://genius.com/Kanye-
west-i-am-a-god-lyrics/

Khaled, DJ. I'm on one. "I'm on one (Featuring Drake, Lil Wayne, & Rick Ross)." We
the Best Forever. Youtube video. We the Best, Terror Squad, Cash Money, Universal
Motown. 2011. Rap Genius. 18 June 2015. http://genius.com/Dj-khaled-im-on-one-
lyrics

The conditioned artist statement VS. The unconditioned artist statement

"A Beautiful Mess"

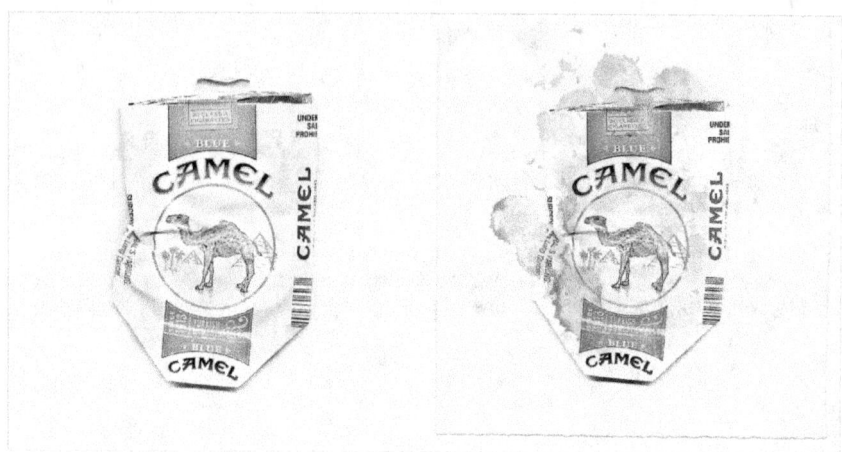

Typical conditioned artist statement
A Beautiful Mess is a play on advertising's ability to make certain products seem more appealing than they truly are. With carefully designed exterior packaging advertising companies deceive, trick, and lure consumers with an aesthetically pleasing trap.

Camel Spill: Watercolors, tea, coffee, and wine mix

Mixed media photography on Somerset Velvet Paper

The conditioned artist statement VS. The unconditioned artist statement

"A Beautiful Mess"

The conditioned artist statement VS. The unconditioned artist statement

"A Beautiful Mess"

Marlboro Spill: Coffee, watercolors, and wine mix

Mixed media photography on Somerset Velvet Paper

The conditioned artist statement VS. The unconditioned artist statement

"A Beautiful Mess"

The conditioned artist statement VS. The unconditioned artist statement

"A Beautiful Mess"

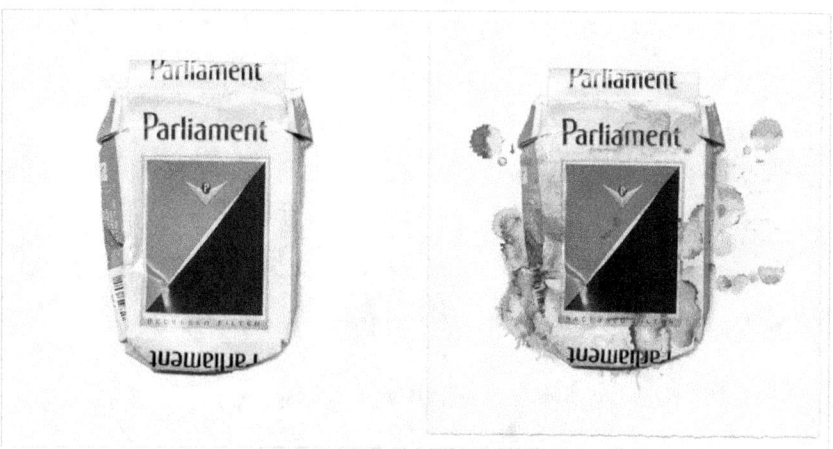

Parliament Spill: Watercolors mix

Mixed media photography on Somerset Velvet Paper

The conditioned artist statement VS. The unconditioned artist statement

"A Beautiful Mess"

The conditioned artist statement VS. The unconditioned artist statement

"A Beautiful Mess"

Playboy Bunny Spill: Watercolors mix

Mixed media photography on Somerset Velvet Paper

The conditioned artist statement VS. The unconditioned artist statement

"A Beautiful Mess"

These are the ingredients that created "A Beautiful Mess":

1. Found cigarette packs on streets and sidewalks

2. Watercolors

3. The Tazo passion tea i drink before bedtime

4. The Barefoot red wine i sip at dinner

5. My morning Coffee

"A Beautiful mess" is an attempt at making something dirty look beautiful. They are mixed media, hand painted, deckle edged prints of found cigarette packs scanned with a flatbed scanner.

This is the short story of how "A Beautiful Mess" was created.

it's 2013, Fall.

it's November. i'm walking to my car. Getting ready to drive to the modern day sweatshop masquerading as my retail job. All of a sudden, in the corner of my eye i spot a crushed Marlboro cigarette pack on the asphalt. it looks interesting, so i walk up to the crushed Marlboro cigarette pack. As i get closer, i notice it's decaying from the natural elements of the world.

its history is imprinted on it. i see that it had been discarded. Stepped on. Ran over by cars, and rained on. But i'm still compelled by it. Find it beautiful, even though it's a dirty product. i pick it up from the asphalt and store it in my bag. i have no idea what to do with it at this time, but i have a good feeling about it. i don't even like cigarettes, but i like the design aspect of it.

i'm drinking 7-11 coffee in my bedroom. it's now a couple of days later, and i'm off from the modern day sweatshop masquerading as my retail job. i want to be productive, since it's a rarity to be off, so i pull the crushed Marlboro cigarette pack from my bag.

i'm sitting in silence, thinking of what to do with the Marlboro cigarette pack, when all of sudden, a short angel flexing the Andy Warhol aesthetic, white wig and black turtle neck, appears on my left shoulder. He says, "Uh… if i were alive today, i would be using computers to create all my artwork since i always wanted to be a robot. it's easy! And i like easy. The time you're living in is perfect, because you have access to all this technology that can create immediate art, and you can be famous for fifteen minutes. Wouldn't that be so, interesting?" i turn to Warhol in his black turtleneck sweater and say, "i have a flatbed scanner that captures images at an insane resolution. i can use that."

i plug in my flatbed scanner to my computer and scan around twenty various compositions of the crushed Marlboro cigarette pack. i then edit and pick the one i intuitively feel is right.

The short Andy Warhol art angel turns and glances at me with approving teary eyes and simply mutters, "Uh, yes…" i continue editing the image to my satisfaction. Once i'm done i find myself scratching my head.

Thinking and asking, "Which direction should i take this image next?" As if here to answer my question another art angel manifests out of thin air. This time it's Jackson Pollock, standing on my right shoulder. He stares me straight in my eye and says, "You want to know which direction you should take this image, son?" i nod energetically and timidly let out, "Yes, sir..." "Make some abstract expressionist spills/paint splatters."

i listen to the Jackson Pollock art angel on my right shoulder, even though i hear the Andy Warhol art angel saying, "Uh... what are you doing... it's already perfect the way it is, with just the logo..."

i open one of my moleskin notebooks. i get a teaspoon and dip it into the 7-11 paper and plastic coffee cup. i then spill the coffee on the teaspoon onto the moleskin pages. i wait for the coffee stained pages to dry. i tear the page out of the moleskin notebook and scan it in.

i glance at the computer screen. i combine the coffee spilled images with the Marlboro pack to see what will happen. Even though the Andy Warhol art angel was a bit skeptical, the image seems to work.

The Jackson Pollock art angel smiles at me and says, "Keep on going son, use some paint."

i reach into my art supplies drawer and get out some watercolors. i spill them onto the moleskin pages. Scan them in and combine them with the crushed Marlboro pack.

i then arrange the composition of the spilled images into something desirable. i think the composition of the spilled images will serve as a good guide/reference image for me when i'm ready to paint the physical prints.

The Andy Warhol art angel, the Jackson Pollock art angel, and i look at the soft glow of the computer screen. All three of us are in awe of what we just created. Both of them simultaneously turn to me and let out music to my ears, "You just gave us the collaboration we could had created when we were alive." The Jackson Pollock art angel says, "it's a pop art meets abstract expressionist hybrid."

"Uh... yes, it's like all the fabulous, cool pop art kids finally decided to eat with the not so cool abstract expressionism kids at the lunch table", the Andy Warhol art angel mutters as he holds his fist to his chin all contemplative like.

The Andy Warhol art angel then says, "This is the beginning of a series of images. You should call it "A Beautiful". "Mess," the Jackson Pollock art angel quickly adds, "A Beautiful Mess."

The biggest grin appears on my face. And i can't stop saying thank you to both the art angels for their divine intervention in my time of creative starvation.

"Uh... find more crushed cigarette packs and do "your thing" will you?" the Andy Warhol art angel says as he disappears. "Make more spills/paint splatters and use various liquids," says the Jackson Pollock art angel as he too disappears.

After both art angels vanish. i continue working on "A Beautiful Mess". i spill watercolors and other liquids. And i find more cigarette packs on the floor around various areas in the city. i scan and combine images and this process created phase one of "A Beautiful Mess".

Fast forward. it's 2014, Summer.

it's July. i'm living in LA now and no longer work at the modern day sweatshop that was masquerading as my retail job. i've been here for six months now, a lot has happened.

i'm in my studio apartment. i'm hand painting one of the images from my series "A Beautiful Mess". it's a 40 x 40 print of a camel cigarette pack on Moab Somerset Velvet Paper with deckled edges. Painting the print is a bit scary, but i'm working of the phase one reference image for this project that already has the composition of the paint splatters laid out for me, so it's not as scary.

i get some Watercolors. Coffee. Red wine and tea. i get some brushes and mix the watercolors. i continue to paint the 40 x 40 print.

i wait till it dries.

i boil some water and make some instant coffee, Nescafe. i take a teaspoon and dip it into the coffee mug. i then spill the contents on the teaspoon onto the appropriate areas of the 40 x 40 print. And wait till it dries. Later at night i drive to Trader Joe's and buy some red wine. A bottle of Charles Shaw Cabernet Sauvignon, to be exact. i swirl the cabernet in this cool wine glass i got from ikea a while back. i sip it. Enjoy it. i get another teaspoon and dip it into the wine glass. i then spill the contents on the teaspoon onto the appropriate areas of the 40 x 40 print. And wait till it dries.

All of a sudden, the Andy Warhol and the Jackson Pollock art angels appear on my shoulders as i'm looking at the finished piece. i say, "you guys made it to LA!"

"Uh..., were omnipresent, we always have an eye on you...you're "a mess" without us. But you've done alright. And your painting the print now! says the Andy Warhol art angel. "i like the progression of your splatters", goes the Jackson Pollock art angel. Before both art angels disappear again they say, "Do us one favor?" i responded, "sure, what?" "Write about us."

And that's what i'm doing right now. Writing at 4:08am on a Friday night about my art angels. A misfit night owl, working on his wildest dreams. i didn't conceive the concept for a "A Beautiful Mess," my art angels did. i was merely a vessel for their genius.

And again, one statement will be good Chinese food that you digest properly. While the other will be not so good Chinese food that gives you food poisoning and elicits puking motions.

And oh yeah, this is the 40 x 40 piece i brought with me to the gallery walk-in i did at Gagosian.

Camel Spill: Watercolors, tea, coffee, and wine mix

Mixed media photography on 40 x 40 Somerset Velvet Paper

My work

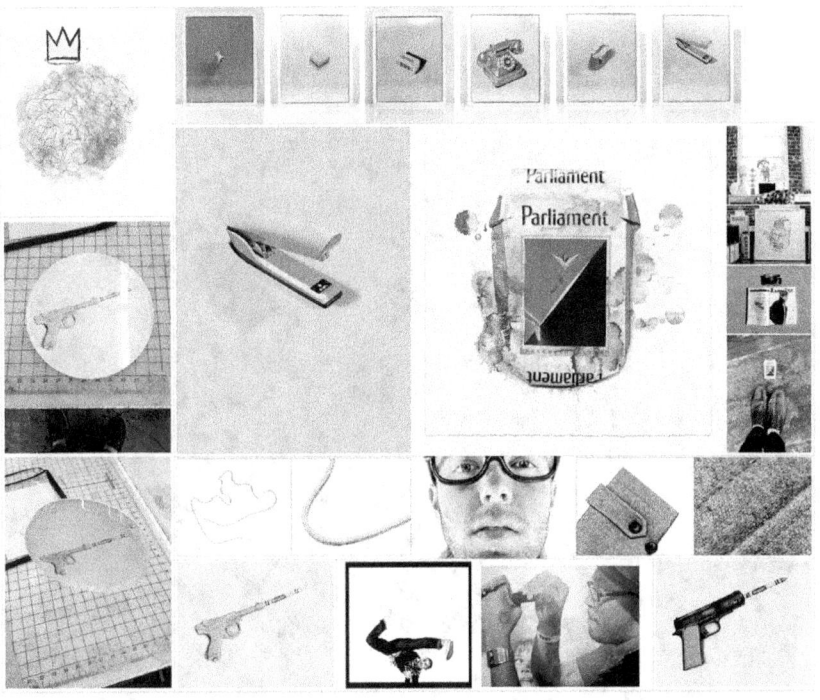

www.victorkphotography.com

15

My Thoughts

(My Thoughts)

My Thoughts

To the person reading this book. i officially finished writing the main portion of this book towards the end of January 2014. i was extremely excited, but was also at a cross road. i wasn't sure what my next step would be. There was option 1. There was option 2.

Option 1
Attempt to publish an unconventional book in a conventional manner. This process was pretty much me submitting my manuscript to various book publishing houses i thought would make a good fit. Writing things like a book market analysis. And other blah blah things...

Option 2
Attempt to publish an unconventional book in an unconventional manner that's rapidly becoming the norm. The self publishing route.

initially, i had went with option 1. i did my research and picked about 30 book publishing houses i thought would make a good fit. i wrote my book's market analysis. i wrote my book's proposal. i wrote my book's intended target audience. And wrote other blah blah things.

it takes about three to six months to review a manuscript. The plan was to wait it out, and if i didn't hear anything by the end of 2015 i would go with option 2. Well the three to six months flew by. And in that time frame i received about 20 rejection letters. Via email. Via snail mail.

And the most interesting thing that happened during that three to six-month time frame wasn't the 20 rejection letters. it was the fact that when i was finding book publishing houses to submit my manuscript to, i came across ones that didn't accept unsolicited book submissions!

i found this discovery pretty ha-ha-ha-ha! because this book is based on breaking the "we don't accept unsolicited submissions" rule.

i feel like someone out there should write a version of this book, but about the book publishing houses, that don't accept unsolicited submissions... Pick ten publishing houses. Pay them a visit with your manuscript in hand. Ask them to take a look. Write short stories about your experiences. Title it, Book Publishing Houses Walk-ins (Unsolicited).

Anyway, it's late 2015 now. December, 16th to be exact. 2016 is right around the corner. And the plan now is to take the self-publishing route. That Macklemore and Ryan Lewis route. "The Label out here, nah they can't tell me nothing. We give it to the people, spread it across the country."

That DJ Khaled route. "They don't want you to win." "They will try to close the door on u, just open it."

That Drake route. "Everybody got a deal, i did it without one."

And lastly, to the person reading this book. if there is only one thing you get out of this book.

Let it be to live life creatively.

in fact, i dare you to do a gallery walk-in yourself. Pick a gallery. Do your research. Make sure your work matches their aesthetic. And make contact with them in "IRL" (in real life).

Don't be rude. Smile tons. Be nice. The thought of it is scary, i know. But i assure you, something magical will happen.

Don't worry, i'm going to live life creatively along with you too. i'll fill you in on my little plan...

So, once this book is officially published and printed. i'm going to pretend to be an intern from a Los Angeles Magazine, and hand deliver copies of to all the galleries i wrote about in the book.

Once i'm there, i'll simply say, "i'm an intern from LA Magazine. i was told to deliver this book to you guys, it's meant for the curator..." Then i'll say, "thank you" and walk out. if they ask me any questions, i'll say, "i'm new, i was just told to make deliveries. i don't know...

This is what i imagine will happen after i've left. They will flip through the book. See the name of their gallery in the contents page. Start buzzing with curiosity. Possibly read their specific chapter or the entire book. And if they make it to this point. And read the following sentence. They will realize that i just checkmated them... and perhaps feel a whirlwind of animated sensations, as they find themselves, floating in a thrilling Hitchcockian suspense at the edge of their seat...

So, that's my little plan.

if i can do it, so can you. i'm awesome, but so are you!

Turn your pain in something beautiful.

Never let go of your child like wonder.

And like Steve Jobs voiced in the 1997 "Think Different" Apple commercial, "Here's to the crazy ones, the misfits. The round pegs in the square holes. The ones who see things differently."

Also most importantly........................

be you even (or especially if) **being** "you" is perceived by others as different or weird.

"30 Hilarious & Inspirational DJ Khaled Quotes." Quotesforbros. Quotesforbros, 17 Dec. 2015. Web. 19 Dec. 2015. <http://www.quotesforbros.com/30-hilarious-inspirational-dj-khaled-quotes/>.

Macklemore. Lewis, Ryan. The Label out here, nah they can't tell me nothing. We give it to the people, spread it across the country. "Cant hold us Ft: Ray Dalton ." The Heist. Youtube video. Macklemore LLC. 2012. Rap Genius. 19 December 2015. http://genius.com/albums/Macklemore-and-ryan-lewis/The-heist

Drake. Everybody got a deal, i did it without one. "Forever Ft: Eminem, Kanye West & Lil Wayne." More Than a Game and Relapse: Refill. Youtube video. Zone 4, Interscope Shady, Aftermath. 2009. Rap Genius. 19 December 2015. http://genius.com/Drake-forever-lyrics/

Apple inc. Los Angeles office of advertising agency TBWA\Chiat\Day. "Here's To The Crazy Ones - Apple's 1997 "Think Different" Commercial." *YouTube*. YouTube, 1997. Web. 19 December 2015. https://www.youtube.com/watch?v=8rwsuXHA7RA

Kedenburg, George, III. "They don't want you to win." http://www.theydontwantyouto.win/ They Don't Want You To Win Generator, n.d Web. 22 Jan. 2016

www.ingramcontent.com/pod-product-compliance
Lightning Source LLC
Chambersburg PA
CBHW072049280526
45788CB00006B/2235